The

H·T·M·L

Programmer's Reference

The

H·T·M·L
Programmer's Reference

Robert Mullen

VENTANA

The HTML Programmer's Reference
Copyright © 1997 by Robert Mullen

Library of Congress Cataloging-in-Publication Data

Mullen, Robert
    The HTML programmer's reference / Robert Mullen.
       p. cm.
    Includes index
    ISBN 1-56604-597-5
    1. HTML (Document markup language) I. Title.
QA76.76.H94M78 1996
005.7'2—dc20   96-42421
                                          CIP

First Edition 9 8 7 6 5 4 3 2 1

Printed in the United States of America

Ventana Communications Group, Inc.
P.O. Box 13964
Research Triangle Park, NC 27709-3964
919.544.9404
FAX 919.544.9472
http://www.vmedia.com

Limits of Liability & Disclaimer of Warranty

Trademarks

Chief Executive Officer
Josef Woodman

**Vice President of
Content Development**
Karen A. Bluestein

Managing Editor
Lois J. Principe

Production Manager
John Cotterman

**Technology Operations
Manager**
Kerry L. B. Foster

**Product Marketing
Manager**
Jamie Jaeger Fiocco

Creative Services Manager
Diane Lennox

Art Director
Marcia Webb

Acquisitions Editor
Neweleen A. Trebnik

Project Editor
Amy E. Moyers

Developmental Editor
Michelle Corbin Nichols

Copy Editor
Bob Campbell

Assistant Editor
Paul Cory

Technical Director
Dan Brown

Technical Reviewers
Patricia McGregor
Daniel I. Joshi

Desktop Publishers
Jaimie Livingston

Proofreader
Alicia Farris

Cover Designer
Alice Whicker

About the Author

Robert Mullen is a HTML author, freelance writer, and editor-at-large living in northern California. Robert has authored or coauthored more than sixteen computer books for personal computer users. Robert also authors a publication for computer publishing professionals called *CoolBlue! Magazine* at http://www.askamerica.com on the World Wide Web.

Richard Jessup contributed the JavaScript portion of this book. As a systems engineer for AT&T, Richard has been involved in computing since the heyday of flight simulation on mainframe computers. Richard also has a background in software development and technical editing.

Acknowledgments

It seems that we rarely find time to praise, but can often find fault in those with whom we work. Creating an instrument of reference like this book can be a daunting task. Always, there are those behind-the-scenes people who make a book such as this—a thing of quality—the recipient of much care and feeding.

It's in that light that I would like to sincerely thank [first] Amy Moyers, Neweleen Trebnik, and Karen Bluestein for their evangelism and support throughout this project. As I sit at an empty desk at the Ventana offices writing this acknowledgment, many others who have helped to turn out this close-to-perfect work will go unmentioned only because I have not had the luxury of meeting them all.

Lots of people leave their mark on a computer book. Outside of originating book content, key contributors added their skills to the fray we have entitled: *The HTML Programmer's Reference*. Many thanks to: Pat McGregor and Daniel Joshi for an outstanding technical edit; Bob Campbell, as always, did a bang-up job fixing my flunkie verbage; Luke Duncan for his technical expertise; Michelle Nichols for her development insights; Jaimie Livingston for his expert desktop design skills; Melanie Stepp for her ability to keep everyone connected effectively; Cheryl Friedman for her Webmaster insights; and Dan Brown for making the content of this book available online.

And a special thanks to Peter and John Kent, authors of the *Official Netscape JavaScript* book (Ventana) for providing the JavaScript appendices.

For all those word warriors who remain unmentioned in these paragraphs, I say thank you for your diligence and skill. Publishing is a partnership of many; the publishing professionals at Ventana play their part well.

Dedication

This book is dedicated to my Elizabeth, the world's foremost wife, who has shown me the virtues of understanding and patience.

And to my daughter Katherine, who is, as the author Pat Conroy once said of one of his own children, "the great gift of my middle age."

Contents

Introduction

The HTML Programmer's Reference is a bit of a blast from the past. You may not recognize this aspect of the book unless you go back as far as I do. The fact is this: It's been some time since a publisher has shown an interest in creating the fastest tools in print—professional references. These books were the boon of professional programmers in the mid-eighties when low-level languages were monsters of learning. "Pure" reference books made it possible for a pro to access the full power and scope of a programming language, and to do so while working in their craft—as they coded.

What is a professional reference? A professional or "pro" reference is simply a book that is designed for speed and agility. These books are optimized so that the reader, with just a modicum of knowledge, can turn to the only page they need to read, then put the book back on the shelf.

In a nutshell, a reference work is not a teaching tool. It's a phone book—a cookbook, if you will. We don't expect to learn or to teach when we use it. I expect you to be able to spell the terms you seek or find them by browsing the "b"s, for example. There is not an index in this book because it's self-indexed, with all HTML and JavaScript entries sorted alpha-numerically.

Part I, the HTML section, is at the core of the HTML 3.2 standards as well as those set by browser makers. This part covers all HTML tags that the HTML author is likely to encounter. To find a particular HTML element (tag), simply thumb through the text to locate the element using the unique alpha-numeric sort.

If you prefer, use the HTML jump table located in Appendix D in lieu of a formal index. Refer to this jump table if you'd rather find the shortcut to the page number you seek.

Part II, the JavaScript section, details information specific to using JavaScript in HTML documents. Don't be suprised to see a lot of mention of HTML and usage examples that detail HTML tags as well. HTML and JavaScript live on the same Web pages, so they are a natural pair to bundle together in this book! Several tables and other appendices are located at the end of this book. Some pertain to HTML, others are exclusive to JavaScript.

Whether it's HTML or JavaScript, get in and get out—fast. That's the beauty of *The HTML Programmer's Reference*.

Who Is This Book For?

Reference books are much more useful to those who know how to look something up—if they don't know what something is called, they obviously can't look it up in a reference book.

The HTML Programmer's Reference is designed for the intermediate-to-advanced reader, and for good reason. Beginning Web authors may not know the name of the tag they seek, so looking up a tag (or an attribute) can be a nightmare. How can you know the name of the tag? Beginners usually are more comfortable working with broad concepts instead of detail items or elements such as HTML tags and attributes. Same deal with budding JavaScript authors.

This book is optimized so that intermediate to advanced readers can go to a topic (the topic name is available to them somehow) to find out how to use that HTML tag, HTML tag attribute, or JavaScript command.

Online Updates Keep You Current

The inexorable truth about the Internet is that it changes constantly. So try as I might to make this book up-to-date, new changes to HTML and JavaScript will come online as *The HTML Programmer's Reference* goes to press. Ventana provides an excellent way to combat this problem and keep the information in this book constantly current—*The HTML Professional Reference Online Updates*. Access this resource at Ventana's World Wide Web site, and you'll find updated material relevant to this book.

To access the Online Updates, aim your browser to *http:// www.vmedia.com/updates.html*.

Part I: HTML

In this part of the book, I detail all HTML tags and attributes that can occur in a Web page. Note that JavaScript is covered in Part II of this book.

You'll find each tag gets its own page, and is followed by descriptions and code usage examples for each tag and attribute combination. The detail level in this book ranks among the most exhaustive and comprehensive references available today on the topics of HTML 2, HTML 3.2, Netscape Navigator 3.0, Microsoft Internet Explorer 3, and Mosaic 2.1.

The following icons denote which HTML standard or browser renders the tag or attribute described on that page:

 HTML 2 icon

 HTML 3.2 icon

 Netscape Navigator 3.0 icon

 Microsoft Internet Explorer 3 icon

 Mosaic 2.1 icon

Part II: JavaScript

The HTML Programmer's Reference includes a part dedicated to JavaScript, a language whose statements are enclosed within <SCRIPT> tags in an HTML file and interpreted along with the HTML by the browser running on a client computer. JavaScript extends HTML by providing such things as additional mouse click responses, improved page manipulation, and a general computation capability which may be used to verify the contents of forms, for example. By allowing correction on the client, there is reduced traffic on the network, reduced load on the server, and better response time for the user.

JavaScript consists of objects with properties which may be manipulated by methods, operators, and functions. Many of the objects and their properties are defined within HTML. JavaScript also includes assignment, declaration, conditional, and loop control statements for general programming purposes. For security reasons, however, it does not have the capability to read and write to the client computer's file system. Its input is limited to that obtained in its objects from HTML forms or its own prompt fields. Its output is limited to the browser's display windows.

Additional Resources

The HTML Programmer's Reference also includes the following resources in the back of the book:

- *Glossary*—An extensive glossary of Internet terms is provided in alphabetical sequence.

- *Appendix A: About the Companion CD-ROM*—This appendix instructs you in the loading and use of the valuable CD-ROM. This CD-ROM contains a complete hyperlinked version of *The HTML Programmer's Reference*.

- *Appendix B: Color Code Tables*—These tables show you all of the colors that can be displayed by most modern browsers. The tables list all colors in two different sorts: by Hex Value and by Color Name.

- *Appendix C: ISO Tables*—Refer to these tables whenever you need to display a non-standard character, or when you simply need to display characters that don't normally occur in the English (U.S.) language. This appendix includes the ISO Latin-1 Character Set as well as the complete ISO Character Set.

■ *Appendix D: Jump Tables*—These jump tables act as an index for you to find the content you need. Each element in the HTML and JavaScript parts are listed alphabetically with page numbers for quick reference.

■ *Appendix E: JavaScript Objects & Arrays*—This appendix lists and describes the various JavaScript objects and arrays, with their associated properties, methods, and event handlers.

■ *Appendix F: JavaScript Properties*—Properties are related to objects and this appendix is a quick summary of the different properties available.

■ *Appendix G: JavaScript Event Handlers*—This appendix provides a summary of the event handlers that are placed within HTML tags. Events are actions a user may take, such as clicking on a button or link, opening or closing a document, and moving focus to and from form elements.

■ *Appendix H: JavaScript Reserved Words*—This appendix lists words you cannot use when naming variables, functions, methods, or objects.

■ *Appendix I: JavaScript Symbol Reference*—This is a quick reference table that will help you identify the different symbols you'll run across while viewing JavaScript.

■ *Appendix J: Finding More JavaScript Information*—The final appendix lists a variety of sources of JavaScript information that you may find helpful.

I

The HTML Reference

This part provides a quick reference to HTML tags and syntax, browser compatibilities, and descriptions and examples of each attribute. For additional references, visit the World Wide Web Consortium's HTML overview at http://www.w3.org/pub/WWW/MarkUp/.

!

Structural Definition

Usage   `<!DOCTYPE: GLOSSARY.HTM 1996/11/27 >`

Description   The ! tag provides a way for the HTML author to place comments into an HTML page. Commented code is not rendered by the browser.

The ! tag can be used to embed messages identifying the document type to a server during a parsing operation.

This tag is not required.

A

Graphics/Links

Usage `<A HREF="http://www.yourname.com">`

Description The A or anchor tag indicates the beginning and the end of a statement containing a hypertext link. A hypertext link can consist of text, an image, or a combination of both.

Using the A tag, the HTML author may link the user to another location within the same HTML document or to another URL.

The A tag requires the use of (at least) the HREF or NAME attributes.

Attributes ## HREF

Usage `<A HREF="http://www.yourname.com/index.htm">`

Description The value of the HREF attribute "refers" to an object such as text internal to the document, text external to the document, a URL internal or external to the document, or an image file.

This attribute is required.

Value URL

NAME

Usage `<A HREF NAME="#Yourname">`

Description The value of the NAME attribute specifies a hotlink to a location within the same document.

This attribute is not required.

Value Text

REL

Usage	`<A HREF REL="Chapter 3">`
Description	The REL attribute directs the browser to link forward to the next link in the same document. This attribute is not required.
Value	Text

REV

Usage	`<A HREF REV="Chapter 2">`
Description	The REV attribute directs the browser to go to the previous link in the same document. This attribute is not required.
Value	Text

TITLE

Usage	`<A HREF TITLE="Home Page">`
Description	The value specified for the TITLE attribute indicates the title of document named in the hyperlink. This attribute is not required.
Value	Text

ADDRESS

Structural Definition

Usage
```
<ADDRESS><I>mur@vmedia.com</I><BR>
This is using the address tag<BR></ADDRESS>
```

Description
The ADDRESS tag directs the browser to render a small body of text into a format resembling an address in an "analog" letter. The text inside the ADDRESS tags is usually rendered in italics. Line breaks in the address text must be manually entered by the HTML author, using either BR or P.

Attributes proposed in the HTML 3 standard set are not supported in HTML 3.2.

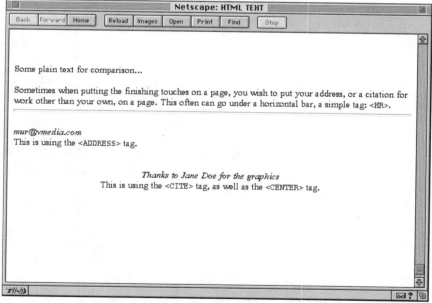

*This is how **ADDRESS** text is rendered by Netscape Navigator 3.0.*

APPLET

Graphics/Links

Usage `<APPLET CODEBASE="MY_APPLET" CODE=MY_APPLET.CLASS WIDTH=200 HEIGHT=30 ALIGN=LEFT>`
`</APPLET>`

Description The APPLET tab directs the browser to embed a Java applet into an HTML document.

Only Java-enabled browsers can render Java applets.

The APPLET tag is ignored by browsers that are not Java-enabled, or if the APPLET tag is not properly used.

Attributes ## ALIGN

Usage `ALIGN=LEFT`

Description The value of the ALIGN attribute specifies alignment of applet as it is displayed by the browser.

This attribute is not required.

Value `ABSMIDDLE`
`ABSBOTTOM`
`BASELINE`
`BOTTOM`
`MIDDLE`
`LEFT`
`RIGHT`
`TEXTTOP`
`TOP`

ALT

Usage   ALT=This text will be displayed in the event the
          browser is not Java-enabled or if the applet cannot
          properly load.

Description The value of the ALT attribute will be displayed (only by
             a Java-enabled browser) in the event the applet cannot
             be loaded.
                 This attribute is not required.

Value   Text

CODE

Usage   CODE=MY_APPLET.CLASS

Description The value of the CODE attribute specifies the class to be
             loaded. If a full URL is not specified, the browser looks
             for the class in the directory of the current HTML docu-
             ment.
                 This attribute is required.

Value   URL

CODEBASE

Usage   CODEBASE="MY_APP"

Description The CODEBASE attribute specifies the base URL of the
             code for the applet. If a full URL is not specified, the
             browser looks for the code in the directory of the current
             HTML document.
                 This attribute is not required.

Value   URL

HEIGHT

Usage   HEIGHT=30

Description   The value specified for the HEIGHT attribute specifies the height of the display area for the Java object. HEIGHT is specified in pixels.
This attribute is required.

Value   Pixels

HSPACE

Usage   HSPACE=10

Description   The value of the HSPACE attribute specifies the number of pixels spaced beside the applet as it is displayed by the browser.
This attribute is not required.

Value   Pixels

NAME

Usage   NAME=MY_APPLET1

Description   The value of the NAME attribute specifies a name for the applet instance. This attribute is required if multiple applets in the same HTML document are expected to interact.
This attribute is not required.

Value   Text

VSPACE

Usage   VSPACE=30

Description   The value of the VSPACE attribute specifies the number of pixels above and below the applet as it is displayed by the browser.
    This attribute is not required.

Value   Pixels

WIDTH

Usage   WIDTH=200

Description   The value of the WIDTH attribute specifies the width of the display area.
    This attribute is required.

Value   Pixels

B

Presentation Formatting

Usage

```
<B>Bolding text, using the <CODE>&lt;B&gt;</CODE> tag, is a nice
way to make text stand out broadly.</B>
```

Description

This tag directs the browser to display the specified text in bold type.

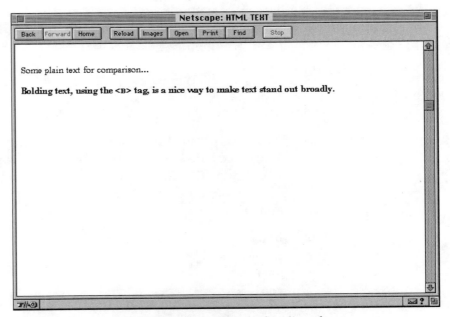

*Compare the second, **BOLD** line of text to the first line of text.*

BASE HREF

Graphics/Links

Usage   The HREF attribute specifies the absolute URL of the home page document.
```
<BASE HREF="http://yourname.com/index.htm">
```

Description   The BASE HREF attribute should be included at the beginning of a page so that a reader can link to the home page even if the reader has bypassed the home page.

Attributes   ## TARGET

Usage   `<BASE TARGET="ABOUT_MY_WEBSITE_WINDOW">`

Description   The TARGET attribute gives the HTML author the ability to create windows that the user can open.
    Note that TARGET is not documented in HTML 2 or 3.2, and that most browsers do not support this uncommon attribute.

Value   _blank
    _parent
    _self
    _top

BASEFONT SIZE

Structural Definition

Usage   `<BASEFONT SIZE=0>`

Description   BASEFONT SIZE directs the browser to specify or respecify the default font size for all text that follows in a document. BASEFONT SIZE specifies the default font size to be zero.

HTML authors use BASEFONT SIZE to set the effective font size to "0" so that following references to font sizing are relative to a base standard on a given page. The default value of this tag is "3."

Value   Digit

BGSOUND SRC

Miscellaneous

Usage   `<BGSOUND SRC="MY_SOUND.WAV">`

Description   The BGSOUND SRC specifies the location (URL) of the sound file to be played.

Attribute **LOOP**

Usage   `<BGSOUND SRC="MY_SOUND.WAV" LOOP=INFINITE>`

Description   The LOOP attribute determines the number of times the audio file is actually played; for example, LOOP=6 plays the file six times. The LOOP=INFINITE value directs the browser to play the sound file indefinitely.

     HTML authors should be aware that the INFINITE value can cause the disk caching mechanism (utilized by some browsers) to fill available hard disk space in a very short period of time.

Value   Digit
         `INFINITE`

BIG

Usage   `<p><BIG>This text is using the <CODE>&lt;BIG&gt;</CODE> tag.`
`</BIG>`

Description   The BIG tag directs the browser to increment font size by one size.

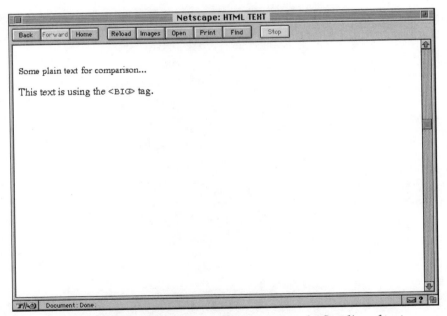

Compare the second line of text, using the BIG tag, to the first line of text.

BLINK

Usage   `<BLINK>Click on a button!</BLINK>`

Description   Directs the browser to blink the specified text. The tag is rendered only by Netscape Navigator.

BLOCKQUOTE

Structural Definition

Usage

```
<BLOCKQUOTE>The <CODE>&lt;BLOCKQUOTE&gt;</CODE> is what you need
here. It keeps the text you write separated to make it stand out
more. End it, and--</BLOCKQUOTE>
<p>then you are back to your regular text.
```

Description

The BLOCKQUOTE tag directs the client browser to indent the specified text on both sides.

BLOCKQUOTE includes a paragraph break before and after the text. Some browsers render BLOCKQUOTE text in italics.

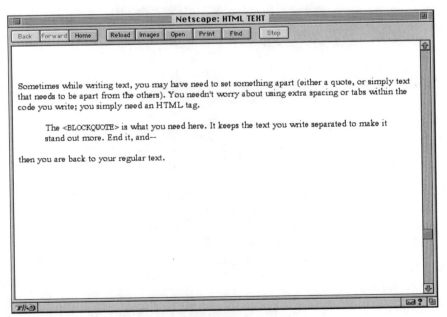

The BLOCKQUOTE tag has indented this text.

BODY

Structural Definition

Usage `<BODY> Your entire HTML document goes here... </BODY>`

Description The BODY tags enclose all text, images, and formatting visible to the user with the exception of document content directed at creating and displaying FRAMES.

Attributes ## ALINK

Usage `<BODY ALINK="BLUE"></BODY>`

Description The ALINK attribute directs the browser to assign a specified color to all links that have been activated when a mouse button is pressed, *but not released*.

Value Color Name

BACKGROUND

Usage `<BODY BACKGROUND="graphic.jpg">`

Description The BACKGROUND attribute specifies a graphics file to be displayed as a background for an entire Web page. The HTML author may direct the browser to display either a JPG or GIF file. Use the smallest bitmaps (in file size and color depth) at hand. Legacy software such as MS Windows 3.1 can be affected by GDI heap depletion if graphics files are both color and size intensive.

Value URL

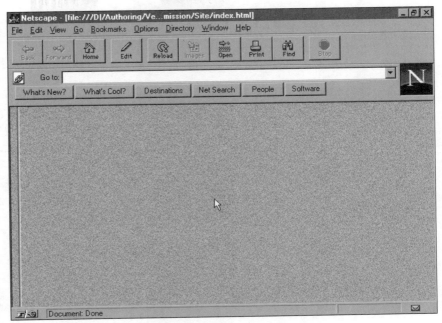

This simple BACKGROUND looks like granite.

BGCOLOR

Usage   `<BODY BGCOLOR="RED">` or `<BODY BGCOLOR=#ff0000>`

Description   The BGCOLOR attribute establishes the background color of an HTML document. Color can be specified using a color's proper name, a hex value, or an RGB value. See the color chart in the back of this book for more detail on colors and color codes.

Value   Color Name

BGPROPERTIES

Usage   `<BODY BACKGROUND="LOGO.GIF" BGPROPERTIES=FIXED></BODY>`

Description   BGPROPERTIES directs the browser to display a background image that does not scroll with the document, giving an impression much like watermarked paper stationary. Only one value can be applied to the BGPROPERTIES attribute: FIXED.

This attribute is different from BODY BACKGROUND in that the image *does not scroll* as the page is scrolled by the viewer when you use this attribute.

Value   `FIXED`

LEFTMARGIN

Usage   `<BODY BACKGROUND="COMPANY_LOGO.GIF" LEFTMARGIN="0">`
`</BODY>`

Description   The LEFTMARGIN attribute directs the browser to set a margin for the left edge of the page, overriding the default margin. Set BODY LEFTMARGIN to "0" (pixels) to place the left margin at the left edge of the page.

Value   Pixels

LINK

Usage   `<BODY BACKGROUND="MY_COMPANY_LOGO.GIF" LINK="RED"`
`BGPROPERTIES=FIXED></BODY>`

Description   The LINK attribute directs the browser to assign a color to all links (in that document) that have not yet been visited. The client browser renders all not-yet-visited links in the specified color unless directed to change that color later in the document.

Value   Color Name

TEXT

Usage
```
<BODY TEXT="MAROON" BACKGROUND="MY_COMPANY_LOGO.GIF">
</BODY >
```

Description
The TEXT attribute directs the browser to assign a color to all text in a document. The client browser renders all text in the specified color unless directed to change that color later in the document.

Value
Color Name

TOPMARGIN

Usage
```
<BODY BACKGROUND="MY_COMPANY_LOGO.GIF"
TOPMARGIN="0"></BODY>
```

Description
The TOPMARGIN attribute directs the browser to set a margin for the top of the page, overriding the default margin. Set BODY TOPMARGIN to "0" (pixels) to set the top margin to the top edge of a page.

Value
Pixels

VLINK

Usage
```
<BODY BACKGROUND="MY_COMPANY_LOGO.GIF" VLINK="BLUE">
</BODY>
```

Description
The VLINK attribute directs the browser to assign a color to all links (in that document) that have been visited. The client browser renders all visited links in the specified color unless directed to change that color later in the document.

Value
Color Name

BR

Presentation Formatting

Usage
```
<ADDRESS>
Your Name<BR>
Your Street Address<BR>
Your City, Your State, Your Zip<BR>
</ADDRESS>
```

Description The BR tag directs the client browser to insert a hard line break. The BR tag can follow text on the same line or it can be on a line all its own, but the result is the same.

Attributes ## CLEAR

Usage `<BR CLEAR=LEFT>This text will be displayed beneath an image and to the left.</BR>`

Description The CLEAR attribute directs the client browser to insert a line break in an HTML document fully clear of any graphics or table that may be in the path of the broken text.

Value
```
LEFT
RIGHT
ALL
NONE
```

CAPTION

Tables

Usage   `<CAPTION>A Caption, <CODE>&lt;CAPTION&gt;</CODE>, can title a table for you.</CAPTION>`

Description   The CAPTION tag places a line of text directly above a table. Captions can be centered and aligned to the TOP (default) or the BOTTOM of the text line.

Attributes   ## ALIGN

Usage   CAPTION ALIGN must be included within the TABLE tags.
`<CAPTION ALIGN="TOP"A Caption, <CODE>&lt;CAPTION&gt;</CODE>, can title a table for you. </CAPTION>`

Description   A caption can be aligned to either the TOP, which is the default, or the BOTTOM of the text line. The ALIGN attribute centers enclosed text on the line.

Value   TOP
BOTTOM

VALIGN

Usage   `<CAPTION VALIGN="TOP">A Caption, <CODE>&lt;CAPTION&gt;`
`</CODE>, can title a table for you. </CAPTION>`

Description   The VALIGN attribute places caption text above or
below a table using the TOP or BOTTOM settings.

Value   TOP
BOTTOM

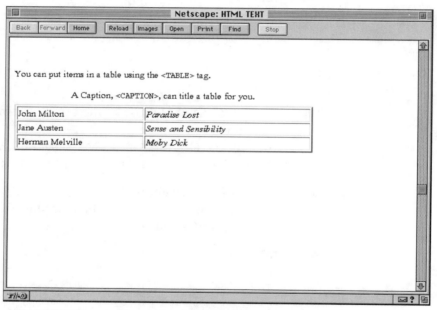

*A **CAPTION** tag can be used as a title for a table.*

CENTER

Usage   `<CENTER>This text will be centered in the browser window.`
`</CENTER>`

Description   The CENTER tag causes text or an image to be centered. Some HTML tags center by default.

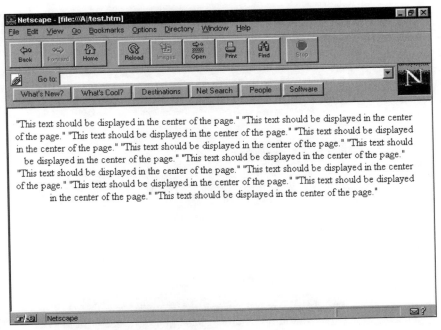

*The **CENTER** tag wraps and centers text.*

CITE

Structural Definition

Usage   `<CITE>Thanks to Jane Doe for the Graphics.</CITE>`

Description   Traditionally, a citation was used as a title or banner on the printed page. In HTML, text placed within CITE tags is italicized by the browser.

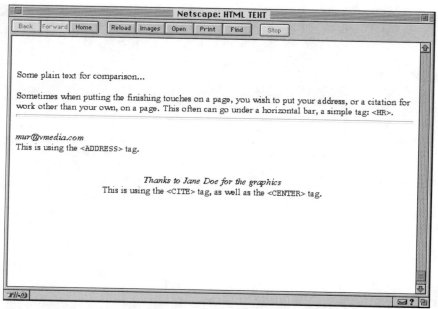

This thank you to Jane Doe has been italicized with the **CITE** *tag.*

CODE

Usage `<CODE>All the examples in this book would be in CODE tags in a HTML document. </CODE>`

Description CODE is used to display commands that should be typed or fragments of the computer code that make up a program. The CODE tag renders text in a monospaced font.

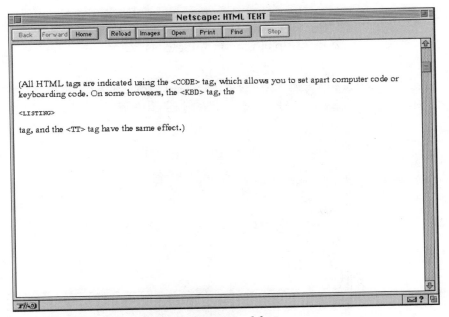

*The **CODE** tag renders text in a monospaced font.*

DD

Structural Definition

Usage
```
<DL>
<DT>John Milton
<DD><I>Paradise Lost</I>
<DD><I>Paradise Regained</I>
<DD><I>Areopagitica</I>
```

Description   The DD tag formats text to be used as a description for a term. The text will appear indented and below the term.

The DD and DT tags are a great way to display terms and descriptions in an online glossary.

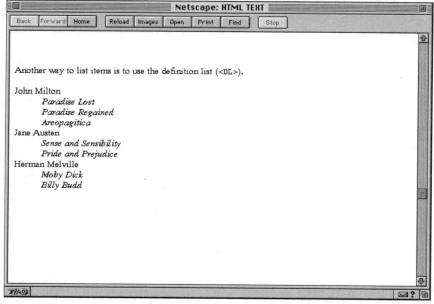

*The **DD** tag, used for the book titles, renders indented description text.*

DFN

Structural Definition

Usage
```
<DD>blah blah.</DD>
<DFN>Using the <CODE>&lt;DFN&gt;</CODE> tag, text will be
displayed below a term's definition.</DFN>
```

Description   DFN means "defining instance." The DFN tag directs the browser to display text beneath a term's definition. Traditional dictionaries often format multiple definitions for a given term in a similar way.

Use the DFN tag to present multiple sub-definitions when they occur.

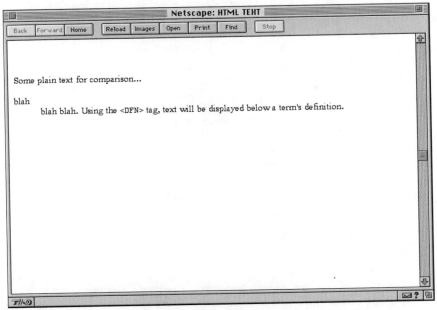

*The **DFN** tag renders multiple description "instances" for a single term.*

DIR

Structural Definition

Usage
```
<DIR TYPE=CIRCLE>
<LI>John Milton
<LI>Jane Austen
<LI>Herman Melville
</DIR>
```

Description
The DIR tag directs the browser to list information in narrow columns, in a table-of-contents format. The DIR tag will truncate text at 20 characters.

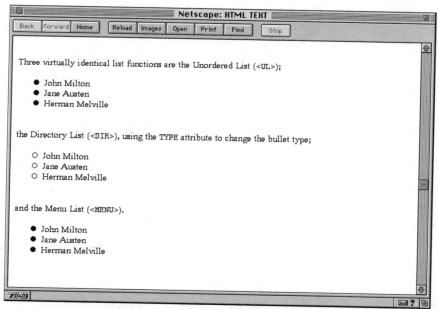

*The **DIR** tag renders multiple line items as a columnar directory.*

DIR TYPE

Lists

Navigator

Usage   `<DIR TYPE=CIRCLE>`

Description   The DIR TYPE attribute directs the client browser to place a bullet of the specified shape at the beginning of a line of DIR text.

The client browser bullets each item in an unordered list with one of three bullets: DISC, CIRCLE, and SQUARE. DISC is the default bullet style. The author can specify any of the three types on any item on a list by specifying different attributes on individual lines inside the LI tags.

Value   CIRCLE
DISC
SQUARE

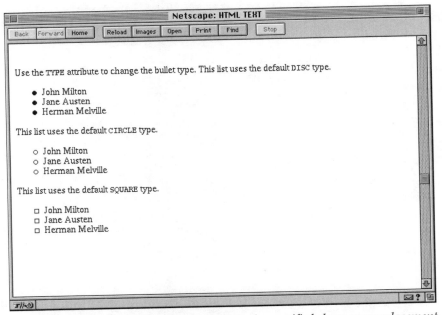

*The **TYPE** attribute for the **DIR** tag renders the specified shape as a replacement for the standard bullets.*

DIV

Structural Definition

Usage

`<DIV ALIGN=CENTER>This text is aligned right.</DIV>`

Description

Divisions are a great way to display paragraphs of text. At Web sites where entire paragraphs must be part of a single hyperlink, the DIV tag can make the syntax quick and easy. Some indexing products parse and display HTML content with entire paragraphs set up as hyperlinks to increase the level of ease for the user.

Attribute **ALIGN**

Usage

`<DIV ALIGN=RIGHT>This text is aligned right.</DIV>`

Description

The ALIGN attribute aligns the specified text. Possible settings are LEFT, RIGHT, and CENTER.

Value

LEFT
RIGHT
CENTER

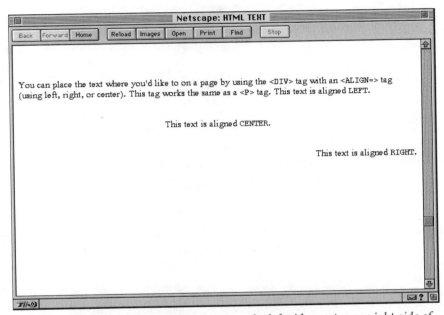

You can place the text where you'd like to on a page by using the <DIV> tag with an <ALIGN=> tag (using left, right, or center). This tag works the same as a <P> tag. This text is aligned LEFT.

This text is aligned CENTER.

This text is aligned RIGHT.

*The **DIV** tag renders a paragraph of text on the left side, center, or right side of the viewing area.*

DL

Usage
```
<DL>
<DT>John Milton<DD><I>Paradise Lost</I>
<DT>Jane Austen<DD><I>Sense and Sensibility</I>
<DT>Herman Melville<DD><I>Moby Dick</I>
</DL>
```

Description
The DL or "Definition List" tag causes text to be rendered as a list of terms. Each term is left-aligned by default, with the relative definition indented.

Attribute ## COMPACT

Usage
```
<DL COMPACT>
<DT>John Milton<DD><I>Paradise Lost</I>
<DT>Jane Austen<DD><I>Sense and Sensibility</I>
<DT>Herman Melville<DD><I>Moby Dick</I>
</DL>
```

Description
The COMPACT attribute causes text to be displayed as a list of terms, in compact format.

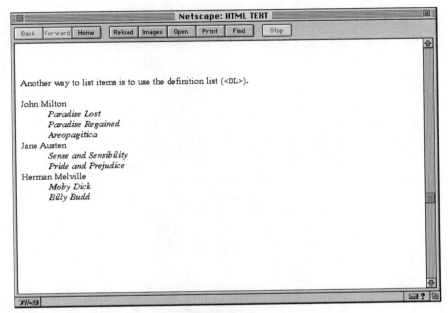

The **DL** tag renders text as a list of definitions.

DT

Lists

Usage
```
<DL>
<DT>John Milton
<DD><I>Paradise Lost</I>
<DD><I>Paradise Regained</I>
<DD><I>Areopagitica</I>
<DT>Jane Austen
<DD><I>Sense and Sensibility</I>
<DD><I>Pride and Prejudice</I>
<DT>Herman Melville
<DD><I>Moby Dick</I>
<DD><I>Billy Budd</I>
</DL>
```

Description   DT means *definition term*. DT renders text as the left-aligned term located just before a definition.

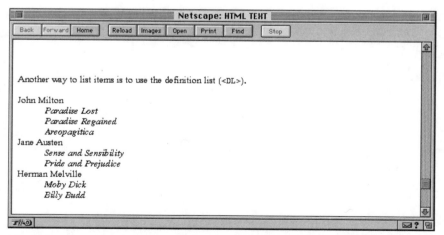

*The **DT** tag renders the author names (John Milton, Jane Austin, and Herman Melville) indented left from the book titles, which have been italicized using the **I** tag.*

EM

Usage   For `<EM>emphasis</EM>`, you may use the `<CODE>&lt;EM&gt;</CODE>` tag

Description   The emphasis or EM tag directs the browser to italicize text. Some legacy browsers may render EM text in bold italics.

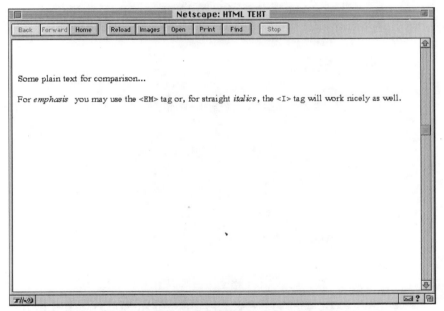

*Netscape Navigator italicizes the text in this illustration with the **EM** tag.*

EMBED

Usage   `<EMBED SRC="MYFILE.JPG">`

Description   The EMBED attribute lets the user edit a display graphic. When the user clicks on the displayed graphic, the *associated* image editing application (which must already be installed on the user's computer) is launched, opening *a copy* of the image file for editing. The image file on the Web page is not edited.

Attributes   ## HEIGHT

Usage   `<EMBED SRC="MYIMAGE.JPG" WIDTH=150 HEIGHT=250>`

Description   The HEIGHT attribute directs the browser to render a specified height for an EMBED object, in pixels.

Value   Pixels

PALETTE

Usage   `<EMBED SRC="MYIMAGE.JPG" PALETTE="FOREGROUND">`

Description   The PALETTE attribute specifies either the FORE-GROUND or BACKGROUND color palette for use during editing.

Value   FOREGROUND
BACKGROUND

SRC

Usage	`<EMBED SRC="MYIMAGE.JPG">`
Description	The SRC attribute specifies the URL of the image or movie to be displayed. This attribute is required.
Value	URL

WIDTH

Usage	`<EMBED SRC="MYIMAGE.JPG" WIDTH=150 HEIGHT=250>`
Description	The WIDTH attribute directs the browser to render a specified width for an EMBED object, in pixels.
Value	Pixels

FONT

Presentation Formatting

Usage `<FONT FACE="Times,Times New Roman,Times Roman" COLOR=Blue FONT SIZE=-1>`

Description The FONT tag directs the browser to render text in specific font type, size, and color. Some attributes of the FONT tag are not recognized by all popular client browsers.

Attributes ## COLOR

Usage `<FONT COLOR=#ff0000>This text will definitely be displayed in Red.</FONT>`

Description The COLOR attribute specifies the color of the text rendered.

Color can be specified in three different ways. In the first method, the HTML author can use the actual color name, such as red or green. The second method allows colors to be specified as RGB values given in percentages of red, green, and blue. The third method is to specify colors in Hex values. Not all browsers utilize "hexadecimal" for specifying colors. Some browsers only recognize the sixteen proper color names or RGB values.

A table defining colors and their hex values can be found at the end of this book.

Value Color Name
Hex Value
RGB Value

FACE

Usage `<FONT FACE="CG Times,New Times Roman,Times"></FONT>`

Description The FACE attribute further directs the browser to render text in a specified font face. Browsers that support this attribute accept the naming of three fonts. If the first named font is not available, the second is utilized, and so on. If none of the three specified fonts are available, the browser uses its own default font.

Value Font Name

SIZE

Usage `<FONT SIZE=7>You</FONT> <FONT SIZE=5>can</FONT> <FONT SIZE=3>change</FONT> <FONT SIZE=1>font</FONT> <FONT SIZE=3>size</FONT> <FONT SIZE=5>with</FONT> <CODE><FONT SIZE=7>&lt;FONT SIZE=1-7&gt;</FONT></CODE>`

Description SIZE further directs the browser to specify the relative size of a font by specifying how much larger or smaller the font should appear. The attribute also increases or decreases the SIZE of the standing BASEFONT setting. Values include 1, 2, 3, 4, 5, 6, and 7—both positive and negative.

Value Digit

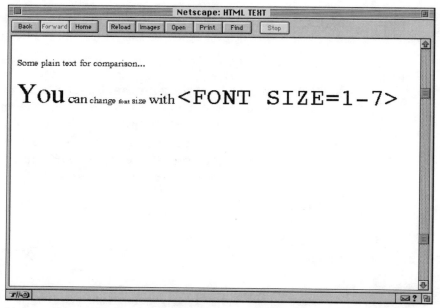

You can change the font size with the FONT SIZE tag.

FORM

Forms

Usage   `<FORM ACTION="COMMENTS.HTM" METHOD="POST"> </FORM>`

Description   The FORM tag denotes the beginning of a section of an HTML document dedicated to accepting input from a user.

     Forms are a collection of inputs located on a single HTML page. Forms can be made up of check boxes, radio buttons, and drop-down lists. Input can also be accepted as text from text boxes filled out by the user.

Attributes   ## ACTION

Usage   `<FORM ACTION="COMMENTS.HTM" METHOD="POST"></FORM>`

Description   The ACTION attribute specifies how input is accepted from the user. Information can be displayed by the browser or sent directly to the server for processing.

Value   URL

ENCTYPE

Usage   `<FORM ENCTYPE="MY_FILE" ACTION="MY_URL" METHOD=POST`

Description   The ENCTYPE attribute specifies the encoding type used to submit data to the server for processing.

Value   URL

METHOD

Usage   `<FORM ENCTYPE="MY_FILE" ACTION="MY_URL" METHOD=POST`

Description   The METHOD attribute directs the browser in how input from a form is processed when the user clicks on the Submit button.

Value   `POST`
             `GET`

TARGET

Usage   `<FORM TARGET="MY_WINDOW" ACTION="MY_URL">`

Description   The TARGET attribute displays a window that contains a FORM's results.

Value   Text
             `_blank`
             `_parent`
             `_self`
             `_top`

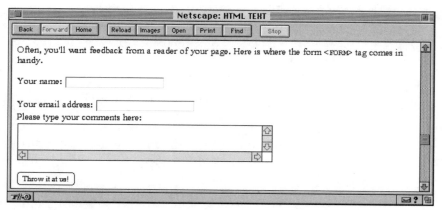

*This is a simple **FORM**.*

FRAME

Frames

Usage `<FRAME NAME="FRAME1">`

Description Netscape first introduced a method of organizing page content with vertical and horizontal dividers called *frames*. The FRAME tag serves to define a single frame as part of a collection of frames called a *frameset*.

Attribute ## FRAMEBORDER

Usage `<FRAME FRAMEBORDER="YES">`

Description The FRAMEBORDER attribute specifies whether the frame's border is visible or invisible. Settings are "YES" (display the border) or "NO" (show no border).

Value YES
NO

FRAMESPACING

Usage `<FRAME FRAMESPACING="5">`

Description The FRAMESPACING attribute gives the HTML author the ability to apply additional space between frames. Specify the amount of space between frames in pixels.

Value Pixels

MARGINHEIGHT

Usage   `<FRAME MARGINHEIGHT=2>`

Description   The MARGINHEIGHT attribute specifies the amount of *vertical* space (in pixels) between an object in a frame and the upper and lower edges of the frame. The browser uses its own judgment if MARGINHEIGHT is not specified.

Value   Pixels

MARGINWIDTH

Usage   `<FRAME MARGINWIDTH=2>`

Description   The MARGINWIDTH attribute specifies the number of pixels of *horizontal* space between an object in a frame and the left or right edges of a frame. If the HTML author doesn't specify a MARGINWIDTH, the browser will make its own judgment and set it for you.

Value   Pixels

NAME

Usage   `<FRAME NAME="MY_FIRST_FRAME">`

Description   The NAME attribute specifies an alphanumeric name for a FRAME window that can be targeted by hyperlinks in other HTML documents. This is an optional attribute.

Value   Text

NORESIZE

Usage   `<FRAME NORESIZE>`

Description   The NORESIZE attribute specifies that a specified frame side cannot be resizable by the user. The HTML author can choose to disallow resizing a frame side or entire frames in a frameset.

     By default, frame-compliant browsers allow all frames to be resized.

Value   —

SCROLLING

Usage   `<FRAME SCROLLING=AUTO>`

Description   The SCROLLING attribute specifies the way you want the contents of a frame to scroll. The YES value allows scrolling the content of a frame. The NO value disallows scrolling of content. The AUTO value allows a vertical scroll bar to be employed in the event that the content of a frame is greater than the viewable area.

     Netscape Navigator and other frame-compliant browsers will use the AUTO value if none other is specified by the HTML author.

Value   YES
         NO
         AUTO

SRC

Navigator   Internet Explorer   Mosaic/ Xmosaic   HTML 3.2

Usage   `<FRAME SRC="MY_LOGO.HTM">`

Description   The SRC attribute directs the browser to display the contents of the specified file. If the file contains frames, these frames will also be displayed in the cell.

Value   URL

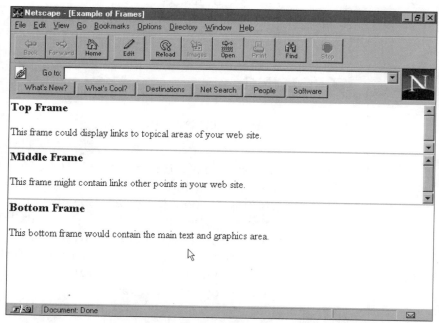

*This figure illustrates three **FRAMES** within a simple **FRAMESET**.*

FRAMESET

Usage
```
<FRAMESET>
<FRAME>
Frame content ...
</FRAME>
</FRAMESET>
```

Description The FRAMESET tag specifies the region of the screen that the browser uses to display frames. It is used instead of the BODY tag if only frames are rendered in a given document.

Attributes **COLS**

Usage Four Examples:
```
<FRAMESET COLS="45">
<FRAMESET COLS="70%">
<FRAMESET COLS="*">
<FRAMESET COLS="45,3*,70%">
```

Description The COLS attribute specifies the height of each frame in pixels or as a percentage of available display space. If the specified value cannot be displayed, the browser renders the FRAMESET using default settings. Values for this attribute must be separated by commas.

The "*" value directs the browser to choose the best column size. Place a number before the "*" value to direct the browser to double available space.

Value Pixels
%
*

ROWS

Navigator Internet Explorer Mosaic/Xmosaic HTML 3.2

Usage   Four Examples:
```
<FRAMESET ROWS=35>
<FRAMESET ROWS="25%">
<FRAMESET ROWS="*">
<FRAMESET ROWS="35,3*,75%">
```

Description   The ROWS attribute specifies the width of each frame in pixels or as a percentage of available display space. If the specified value cannot be displayed, the browser renders the FRAMESET using default settings. Values used with this attribute must be separated by commas.

The "*" value directs the browser to choose the best row size. Place a number before the "*" value to direct the browser to double its assignment of space based on its own assessment of available space.

Value   Pixels

%

*

H1

Structural Definition

Usage `<H1>This is using the <CODE>&lt;H1&gt;</CODE> tag.</H1>`

Description Headings are a typographical convention designed to aid in the hierarchical organization of text in a document. H1 specifies the use of the first-level heading in a body of text. There are a total of six heading levels, numbered one through six.

Attributes ## ALIGN

Usage `<H1 ALIGN="CENTER">This heading text will be centered.</H1>`

Description The ALIGN attribute directs the browser to align text in this heading level LEFT, CENTER, or RIGHT.

Value LEFT
CENTER
RIGHT

Netscape: HTML TEXT

Back Forward Home   Reload Images Open Print Find   Stop

This is using the `<H1>` tag.

Some plain text for comparison...

Document: Done.

---

*This figure illustrates an example of text rendered by the **H1** tag.*

H2

Structural Definition

Usage   `<H2><IMG SRC="YOUR.GIF"> Table of Contents</H2>`

Description   Headings are a typographical convention designed to aid in the hierarchical organization of text in a document. H2 specifies the use of the second-level heading in a body of text. There are a total of six heading levels, numbered one through six.

Attributes   ## ALIGN

Usage   `<H2 ALIGN="CENTER">Your heading text goes here ... </H2>`

Description   The ALIGN attribute directs the browser to align text in this heading level LEFT, CENTER, or RIGHT.

Value   `LEFT`
`CENTER`
`RIGHT`

H3

Usage   `<H3>Your heading text goes here ... </H3>`

Description   Headings are a typographical convention designed to aid in the hierarchical organization of text in a document. H3 specifies the use of the third-level heading in a body of text. There are a total of six heading levels, numbered one through six.

Attribute   ## ALIGN

Usage   `<H3 ALIGN="RIGHT">Your third heading will align to the right... </H3>`

Description   The ALIGN attribute directs the browser to align text in this heading level LEFT, CENTER, or RIGHT.

Value   `LEFT`
`CENTER`
`RIGHT`

H4

Usage   `<H4>Your heading 4 text goes here ... </H4>`

Description   Headings are a typographical convention designed to aid in the hierarchical organization of text in a document. H4 specifies the use of the fourth level heading in a body of text. There are a total of six heading levels, numbered one through six.

Attribute   **ALIGN**

Usage   `<H4 ALIGN="RIGHT">Your Heading 4 text goes here</H4>`

Description   The ALIGN attribute directs the browser to align text in this heading level LEFT, CENTER, or RIGHT.

Value   LEFT
        CENTER
        RIGHT

H5

Usage   `<H5>Put more text here ... </H5>`

Description   Headings are a typographical convention designed to aid in the hierarchical organization of text in a document. H5 specifies the use of the fifth-level heading in a body of text. There are a total of six heading levels, numbered one through six.

Attribute   **ALIGN**

Usage   `<H5 ALIGN="LEFT">Your fifth heading text will be aligned left. </H5>`

Description   The ALIGN attribute directs the browser to align text in this heading level LEFT, CENTER, or RIGHT.

Value   LEFT
CENTER
RIGHT

H6

Structural Definition

Usage   `<H6>Your Heading 6 text goes here ... </H6>`

Description   Headings are a typographical convention designed to aid in the hierarchical organization of text in a document. H6 specifies the use of the sixth-level heading in a body of text. There are a total of six heading levels, numbered one through six.

Attribute   ## ALIGN

Usage   `<H6 ALIGN="CENTER">This heading text will be centered</H6>`

Description   The ALIGN attribute directs the browser to align text in this heading level LEFT, CENTER, or RIGHT.

Value   `LEFT`
`CENTER`
`RIGHT`

HEAD

Structural Definition

Usage
```
<HEAD >
<META CONTENT="MOZILLA">
</HEAD>
```

Description   The HEAD tag encloses lines of information that refer to the document content. META and HEAD lines are enclosed in the HEAD tags. A closing tag is required.

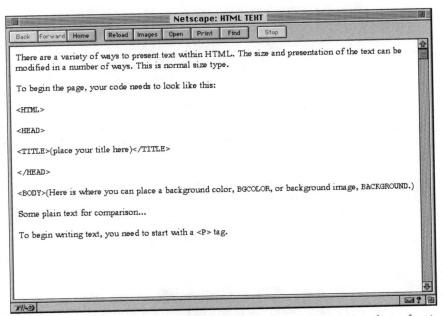

By using the HEAD tag, you're able to enclose lines of information that refers to document content.

HR

Usage   `<HR>`

Description   The HR stands for Horizontal Rule. A Horizontal Rule separates content from other content in an HMTL document. The HR tag draws a horizontal rule or line shaded with a 3D look.
The HR tag needs no closing tag.

ALIGN

Attribute

Usage   `<HR ALIGN="LEFT">`

Description   The HR ALIGN tag/attribute combination draws a horizontal rule and aligns the rule to the LEFT, the CENTER, or the RIGHT of a document. The HR ALIGN tag/attribute combination needs no closing tag.

Value   LEFT
CENTER
RIGHT

COLOR

Usage   `<HR COLOR="GREEN">`

Description   The COLOR attribute draws a 3D horizontal rule of a specified color, named as a color or as a Hex .

Value   Text

NOSHADE

Usage   `<HR NOSHADE>`

Description   The NOSHADE attribute draws a horizontal rule, but with no 3D shading.

Value   —

SIZE

Usage   `<HR SIZE="5">`

Description   The SIZE [height] can be specified in pixels.

Value   Pixels

WIDTH

Usage   `<HR WIDTH="90%">`

Description   The width of the rule can be specified either as a number of pixels or as a percentage of the available viewing space. For example, the HTML author could specify a rule 500 pixels wide or one occupying 80 percent of the available viewing space.

Value   Pixels
              %

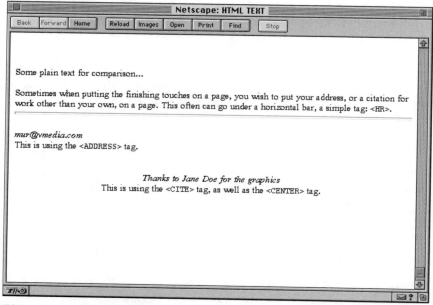

This rule, created with the HR tag, is being used to separate the body of this web page from the address and citation lines.

HTML

Structural Definition

Usage
```
<HTML>
<BODY>
<H2>This is an HTML document with only one heading line it it.
</H2>
</BODY>
</HTML>
```

Description   The HTML tag indicates the beginning and the end of an HTML document. All other tags must be placed within the HTML tags or they will be ignored by the client browser.

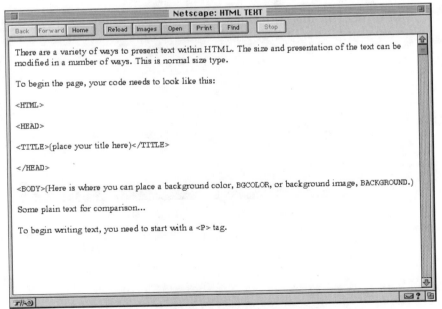

The HTML tag indicates the beginning and the end of an HTML document.

I

Presentation Formatting

Usage   for straight <I>italics</I>, the <CODE><I></CODE> tag will work nicely

Description   Text within the I, or Italic, tag is rendered in italics.

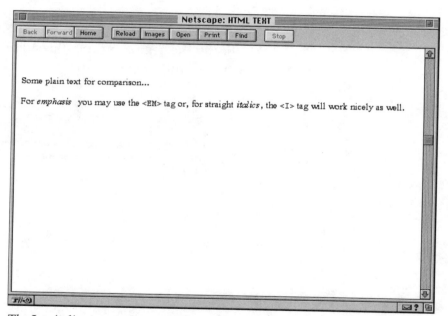

*The **I** or italics tag renders text in italics.*

IMG SRC

Graphics/Links

Usage `<IMG SRC=" MYFILE.GIF ">`

Description The IMG SRC tag directs the browser to display a still image or related text, specified as a filename. Although IMG is often referred to as a stand-alone tag, the SRC attribute is required in order to specify the image file (URL) to be displayed.

Value URL

Attribute **ALIGN**

Usage `<IMG SRC="MYFILE.GIF" ALIGN=CENTER>`

Description The value of the ALIGN attribute specifies the way the image is aligned in its space.

Value ABSMIDDLE
ABSBOTTOM
BASELINE
BOTTOM
CENTER
MIDDLE
LEFT
RIGHT
TEXTTOP
TOP

ALT

Usage   `<IMG SRC=" MYFILE.GIF " ALT="My Message">`

Description   The ALT attribute substitutes specified text if the specified image cannot be displayed by a browser, if the user has in-line images turned off to load pages faster, or if the transfer is interrupted before the images load on pages where the HTML author has used the HEIGHT and WIDTH attributes.

Value   Text

BORDER

Usage   `<IMG SRC="MYFILE.GIF" BORDER="3">`

Description   The BORDER attribute draws a border around the specified image, specified in pixels.

Value   Pixels

CONTROLS

Usage   `<IMG SRC="MYFILE.GIF" DYNSRC="MYFILE.AVI" CONTROLS>`

Description   The CONTROLS attribute directs the browser to display a VCR-like set of controls under moving images being presented if used in conjunction with the DYNSRC attribute.

Value   —

DYNSRC

Usage   `<IMG SRC="IMAGE.GIF" DYNSRC="MOVIE.AVI">`

Description   The value of the DYNSRC attribute specifies the URL of a video, AVI clip, or VRML world to be rendered in its own window. Your browser has to be able to render images inline for the DYNSRC attribute to be rendered properly.

Value   URL

HEIGHT

Usage   `<IMG SRC="MYFILE.GIF" HEIGHT=153>`

Description   A graphics file need not be permanently resized to be displayed in varying contexts; however, the HTML author may direct the browser to resize with the number of pixels specified by the value of the HEIGHT attribute.

Value   Pixels

HSPACE

Usage   `<IMG SRC=" MYFILE.GIF " HSPACE=10>`

Description   The HTML author can specify how much space (in pixels) resides on the left and right of an image with the HSPACE attribute.

Value   Pixels

ISMAP

Usage
```
<A HREF="MYMAP.MAP">
<IMG SRC="MYFILE.GIF" ISMAP>
</A>
```

Description IMG SRC ISMAP is used, in conjunction with A HREF, to insert a picture into an HTML document, and to further direct the client browser to refer to the specified image map (specified as a URL) when the user clicks on the image.

Value URL

LOOP

Usage
```
<IMG SRC="MYFILE.GIF" DYNSRC="MYFILE.AVI"
LOOP=INFINITE>
```

Description LOOP directs the browser to play the moving image file perpetually (LOOP=INFINITE) or a specified number of times (example: LOOP="5").

Value Binary
INFINITE

LOWSRC

Usage `<IMG SRC="MYFILE.JPG" LOWSRC="MYFILE.GIF">`

Description The added LOWSRC attribute is used to specify a low-resolution image intended to be utilized as a *link* to a higher-resolution image.

Value URL

START

Usage   `<IMG SRC=" MYFILE.GIF " DYNSRC="MYMOVIE.AVI" START=MOUSEOVER>`

Description   The START attribute tells the browser when to begin display of the specified image.
      The FILEOPEN value directs the browser to begin display of any moving image files when the HTML document is first opened by the user.
      The MOUSEOVER value directs the browser to play the moving image file when the mouse is moved over a representative still image.

Value   `FILEOPEN`
            `MOUSEOVER`

USEMAP

Usage   `<IMG SRC="MYFILE.GIF" USEMAP "#MY_MAP.MAP">`

Description   The USEMAP attribute specifies that a picture is a client-side image map and further specifies a MAP (a URL with a prefix of "#") to be used when the user clicks on the image.

Value   URL

VSPACE

Usage   `<IMG SRC=" MYFILE.GIF " VSPACE=5>`

Description   The VSPACE attribute provides a means of creating blank (clear) space over or under an image, specified in pixels.

Value   Pixels

WIDTH

Usage `<IMG SRC="MYFILE.GIF" WIDTH=575>`

Description A graphics file need not be permanently resized to be displayed in varying contexts; however, the HTML author may direct the browser to resize with specified image WIDTH attributes, in pixels. If you use the WIDTH and HEIGHT attributes to resize a picture and a reader has a browser that does not support it, your page will not display as intended.

Value Pixels

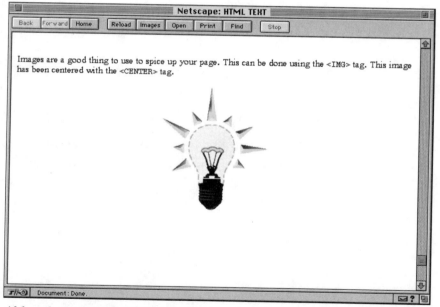

*Although **IMG SRC ALIGN=MIDDLE** can be used to render the specified image in the center of the page, this image has been centered by simply using the CENTER tag to enclose the IMG tag.*

INPUT

Usage	See attributes for examples of usage.
Description	The INPUT tag creates an input object used in a form. By default, the tag creates a text object.

Attribute

LOOP

Usage	`<IMG SRC="MYFILE.GIF" DYNSRC="MYFILE.AVI" LOOP=INFINITE>`
Description	LOOP directs the browser to play the moving image file perpetually (LOOP=INFINITE) or a specified number of times (example: LOOP="5").
Value	Binary INFINITE

LOWSRC

Usage	`<IMG SRC="MYFILE.JPG" LOWSRC="MYFILE.GIF">`
Description	The LOWSRC attribute is used to specify a low-resolution image intended to be utilized as a link to a higher-resolution image.
Value	URL

NAME

Usage `<INPUT NAME="ADDRESS_1">`

Description The NAME attribute specifies the label assigned to a forms object. NAME is a required attribute of the INPUT tag when a text box is further defined with additional attributes.

Value Text

NAME ALIGN

Usage `<INPUT NAME="ADDRESS_1" TYPE=IMAGE ALIGN=MIDDLE>`

Description ALIGN specifies that text will be aligned to the TOP, the MIDDLE, or the BOTTOM of a preceding image.

Value TOP
MIDDLE
BOTTOM

NAME CHECKED

Usage `<INPUT NAME="CHECKBOX_1" TYPE=CHECKBOX CHECKED=FALSE>`

Description The CHECKED tag sets a check box or radio button to "true" or "checked" by default.

Value TRUE
FALSE

NAME MAXLENGTH

Usage	`<INPUT NAME="TEXTBOX1" MAXLENGTH="50">`
Description	The MAXLENGTH attribute specifies how many characters a user may enter into a text box.
Value	Pixels

NAME SIZE

Usage	`<INPUT NAME="TEXTBOX_1" SIZE="35">`
Description	The SIZE attribute gives the HTML author a way to specify the *visible* size (length in characters) of a text box.
Value	Characters

NAME SRC

Usage	`<INPUT NAME="ADDRESS_1" TYPE=IMAGE SRC="MYFILE.GIF">`
Description	Used only in conjunction with INPUT NAME TYPE=IMAGE, the SRC attribute (a URL) directs the browser to display the specified image.
Value	URL

NAME TYPE

Usage   `<INPUT NAME="CHECKBOX_1" TYPE=CHECKBOX>`

Description   TYPE specifies the form control type.

Value   CHECKBOX
IMAGE
PASSWORD
RADIO
RESET
SUBMIT
TEXT

NAME VALUE

Usage   `<INPUT NAME="CHECKBOX_1" TYPE=CHECKBOX VALUE=1>`

Description   VALUE specifies text or Boolean information that occupies a text box *before* the user enters information. The Working Syntax specifies that a check box is displayed, and that the default VALUE is to be 1 or ON.

Value   Text

START

Usage   `<IMG SRC="MYFILE.GIF" DYNSRC="MYMOVIE.AVI" START=MOUSEOVER>`

Description   The START attribute tells the browser when to begin display of the specified image.
       The FILEOPEN value directs the browser to begin display of any moving image files when the HTML document is first opened by the user.

The MOUSEOVER value directs the browser to play the moving image file when the mouse is moved over a representative still image.

Value   FILEOPEN
         MOUSEOVER

USEMAP

Usage   `<IMG SRC="MYFILE.GIF" USEMAP "#MY_MAP.MAP">`

Description   The START attribute tells the browser when to begin display of the specified image.

The FILEOPEN value directs the browser to begin display of any moving image files when the HTML document is first opened by the user.

The added USEMAP attribute specifies that a picture is a client-side image map and further specifies a MAP (a URL with a prefix of "#") to be used when the user clicks on the image.

Value   URL

VSPACE

Usage   `<IMG SRC="MYFILE.GIF" VSPACE=5>`

Description   The START attribute tells the browser when to begin display of the specified image.

The FILEOPEN value directs the browser to begin display of any moving image files when the HTML document is first opened by the user.

The added VSPACE=" ... " attribute provides a means of creating blank (clear) space over or under an image, specified in pixels.

Value   Pixels

WIDTH

Usage `<IMG SRC="MYFILE.GIF" WIDTH=575>`

Description A graphics file need not be permanently resized to be displayed in varying contexts; however, the HTML author may direct the browser to resize with specified image WIDTH attributes, in pixels. If you use the WIDTH and HEIGHT attributes to resize a picture and a reader has a browser that does not support it, your page will not display as intended.

Value Pixels

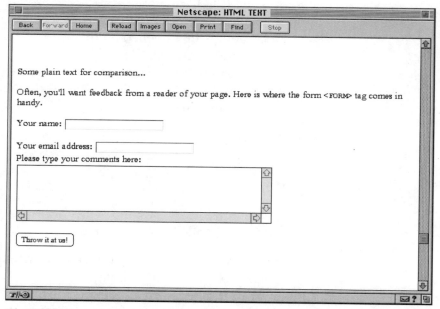

*The **INPUT** tag creates user input objects. This form uses 3 text input objects and one submit input object, all created with the NAME TYPE attribute.*

ISINDEX

Forms

Usage   `<ISINDEX>`

Description   ISINDEX indicates to a server that a document is searchable. The ISINDEX tag displays a text box for the entry of search keywords and directs the client browser to display the following message along with the text box: "You can search this index. Type the keyword(s) you want to search for: "

Text submitted with this rudimentary form is posted back to the page's URL as a query or to a CGI script. FORM is more commonly used today to collect information from the user.

Attribute   ## ACTION

Usage   `<ISINDEX ACTION="SEARCH">`

Description   The ACTION attribute of the ISINDEX tag sends submitted text to a specified gateway (CGI) program.

Value   Text

PROMPT

Usage   `<ISINDEX PROMPT="Why not use your own text prompt instead?">`

Description   The PROMPT attribute of the ISINDEX tag gives the author a way to substitute a customized text message for the default text message.

Value   Text

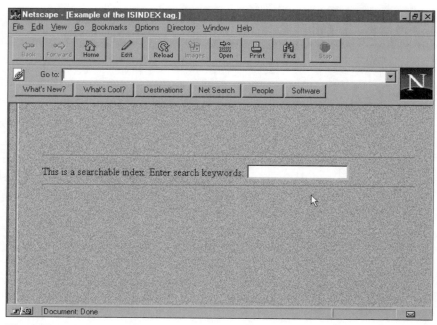

*The **ISINDEX** tag renders a text box used for basic keyword searches.*

KBD

Structural Definition

Usage   `<KBD>This text will look like classic typewriter text. </KBD>`

Description   The KBD tag directs the browser to render specified text in a monospaced font, in bold. The KBD tag is useful in presenting text that is meant to look like that made with a typewriter. In most browsers it will display in the same font as CODE.

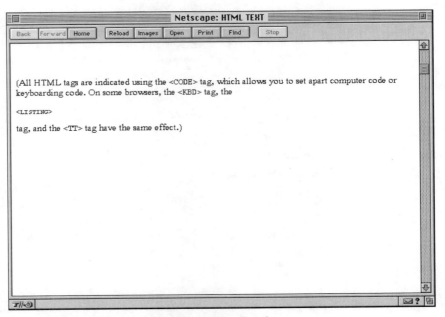

*The **KBD** tag renders text in a "typewriter" style.*

LI

Usage
```
<UL>
<LI>This is a single list item. </LI>
</UL>
```

Description The LI tag renders text as an item on a list. Lists can be unordered, ordered, or bulleted [the default].

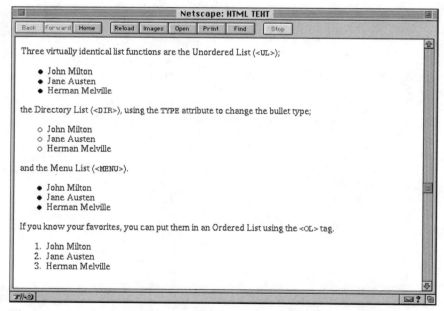

*The **LI** tag renders text as a line item on an unordered, ordered, or bulleted [the default] list.*

Attribute **TYPE**

Usage
```
<UL>
<LI TYPE="A">This item will be ordered with uppercase
letters. </LI>
</UL>
```

Description The value of the TYPE attribute replaces numbers on a numbered list with different characters:

A   uppercase letters
a   lowercase letters
I   uppercase Roman numerals
i   lowercase Roman numerals

Value
```
A
a
I
I
```

VALUE

Usage
```
<OL>
<LI VALUE="4">The first item on this list will be item
number four!</LI>
<LI>This will be item number five!</LI>
<LI>This will be item number six!</LI>
</OL>
```

Description The VALUE attribute specifies the first digit to be used in a numbering sequence.

Value Digit

LINK

Graphics/Links

Usage   `<LINK HREF="MYFILE.HTM">`

Description   The LINK tag specifies the destination URL named in a hotlink. A LINK can specify a point in the same document or the URL of another document. The LINK tag must be used inside HEAD tags.

Attribute   **HREF**

Usage   `<LINK HREF="HTTP://WWW.MY_COMPANY.COM/MYFILE.HTM">`

Description   The HREF attribute of the LINK tag hotlinks the user to another specified HTML document when the user clicks on the hotlink.

Value   URL

ID

Usage   `<LINK ID="MYFILE.HTM">`

Description   LINK ID gives the HTML author the ability to specify a named file (URL) or text as a hypertext link to another document (or another point in the same document).

Value   URL

REL

Usage `<LINK REL="MYFILE.HTM">`

Description The LINK REL tag/attribute combination directs the browser to link *forward* to the next page or link in a document. The LINK REL tag/attribute combination is useful in creating slide show–like presentations in very long documents.

Value URL

REV

Usage `<LINK REV="/MYFILES/MYFILE.HTM">`

Description Like the LINK REL tag/attribute combination, LINK REV provides the HTML author with a means of managing links inside large documents.

The LINK REV tag/attribute combination directs the browser to go to the previous link in the same document.

Value URL

TITLE

Usage `<LINK TITLE="Page 10 of 156">`

Description As originally intended, the TITLE attribute indicates the title of the document named in the link. The TITLE attribute also provides a way to place a string of text in the LINK syntax that is not visible to the browser.

Value URL

LISTING

Structural Definition

Usage

```
<LISTING>This text will be  displayed in a fixed width font.
</LISTING>
```

Description

The LISTING tag renders text in a monospaced font, as if it were printed on an old typewriter or computer printout. Some browsers no longer recognize LISTING, which has been superseded by CODE or KBD.

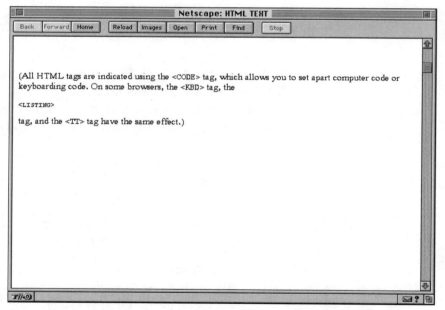

*The **LISTING** tag is yet another HTML tag that renders text in a fixed-width font.*

MAP • **81**

MAP

Graphics/Links

Usage See attributes for an example of usage.

Description MAP specifies information about a client-side image map. The AREA tag is required in order to specify the hot spot regions.

Attribute **NAME**

Usage `<MAP NAME="MY_MAP_NAME">`

Description This attribute allows the HTML author to label the MAP with a name.

Value Text

MARQUEE

Usage See attributes for examples of usage.

Description The MARQUEE tag scrolls text across an area of the available viewing area.

Attribute ALIGN

Usage `<MARQUEE ALIGN=TOP>This text will be aligned along the top of the Marquee.</MARQUEE>`

Description The ALIGN attribute of the MARQUEE tag aligns scrolling text to the TOP, the MIDDLE, or the BOTTOM of the marquee.

Value TOP
BOTTOM
MIDDLE

BEHAVIOR

Usage `<MARQUEE BEHAVIOR=ALTERNATE>This text will bounce around a bit!</MARQUEE>`

Description The BEHAVIOR attribute directs the browser to handle the text according to a specified method once the text has been rendered on the page. With SLIDE, the text slides onto the document and then stops at the margin. With ALTERNATE, the text bounces from side to side. With SCROLL, the text repeatedly scrolls across the page.

Value   SLIDE
             ALTERNATE
             SCROLL

BGCOLOR

Usage   `<MARQUEE BGCOLOR="ORANGE">This Marquee background will be orange in color!</MARQUEE>`

Description   BGCOLOR specifies the background color of a marquee, in RGB, Hex Value format, or in English language expressions such as "RED" and "BLUE."

Value   Color Name
             Hex Value

DIRECTION

Usage   `<MARQUEE DIRECTION=LEFT>This marquee text will scroll to the left in direction.</MARQUEE>`

Description   DIRECTION specifies the actual direction of the scrolling.

Value   LEFT
             RIGHT

HEIGHT

Usage   `<MARQUEE HEIGHT=10%>This text occupies 10% of the screen.</MARQUEE>`

Description   HEIGHT specifies the height of the marquee, in pixels or a percentage of the visible page.

Value   Pixels
             %

HSPACE

Usage   `<MARQUEE HSPACE=15>This text is bordered by fifteen pixels. </MARQUEE>`

Description   HSPACE specifies the amount of clear space adjoining a marquee, to the left and the right, in pixels.

Value   Pixels

LOOP

Usage   `<MARQUEE LOOP=10>This text will scroll ten times. </MARQUEE>`

Description   LOOP specifies the number of times a marquee will be scrolled. MARQUEE text can be scrolled for a specified number of times with (for example) MARQUEE LOOP=5 or indefinitely with MARQUEE LOOP=INFINITE or MARQUEE LOOP= –1.

Value   Digit
`INFINITE`

SCROLLAMOUNT

Usage   `<MARQUEE SCROLLAMOUNT=10>This text will be followed by ten pixels of space.</MARQUEE>`

Description   SCROLLAMOUNT specifies the space after each successive scrolling of text, in pixels.

Value   Pixels

SCROLLDELAY

Usage   `<MARQUEE SCROLLDELAY=5>This text will scroll every five seconds.</MARQUEE>`

Description   SCROLLDELAY specifies the amount of time that will pass between scrolling actions, given in milliseconds.

Value   Digit

VSPACE

Usage   `<MARQUEE VSPACE=2>This text has two pixels above and below it.</MARQUEE>`

Description   The VSPACE attribute is used to specify the amount of clear space adjoining a marquee, above and below, in pixels.

Value   Pixels

WIDTH

Usage   `<MARQUEE WIDTH=90%>This MARQUEE text will occupy 90% of the available viewing area.</MARQUEE>`

Description   The WIDTH attribute specifies the width of the marquee, in either pixels or a percentage of the viewable page.

Value   Pixels
%

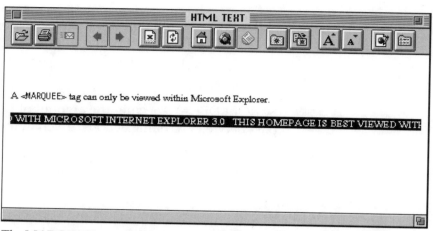

*The **MARQUEE** tag scrolls text across the screen in several ways.*

MENU

Structural Definition

Usage
```
<MENU>
<LI>John Milton
<LI>Jane Austin
<LI>Herman Melville
</MENU>
```

Description The MENU tag specifies the start of a MENU list.

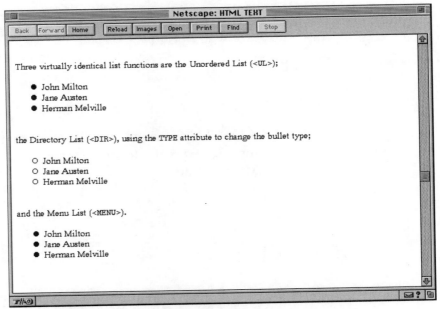

*The **MENU** tag creates a bulleted list, or "menu."*

META

Graphics/Links

Usage

```
<META HTTP-EQUIV="REFRESH" CONTENT="2" URL="HTTP://
WWW.MYSITE.COM/INDEX.HTM">
```

Description The META tag is used to indicate special instructions for the client browser or a server performing a parsing operation. Other text can be included to denote date of creation, etc.

Search engines may post information specified by the META tag.

The META tag must be placed as part of the HEAD in an HTML document.

Attribute ## CONTENT

Usage `<META HTTP-EQUIV="REFRESH" CONTENT=2>`

Description The CONTENT attribute provides information related to the topic (or type of information) specified with the NAME attribute.

Value Text

HTTP-EQUIV

Usage `<META HTTP-EQUIV="REFRESH" CONTENT=5>`

Description HTTP-EQUIV directs the browser to make requests of the server in order to perform various HTTPD functions — within the capabilities of the client. REFRESH is just one value that directs the client to re-post the URL named or the current document (default).

Value   REFRESH
          Other values for this attribute vary greatly based on the
          server and client software in use. Check your server and
          browser documentation for useful HTTPD functions.

NAME

Usage   `<META NAME="Publisher" CONTENT="Ventana">`

Description   The NAME attribute indicates the *type* of information
          specified by the CONTENT attribute.

Value   Text

URL

Usage   `<META HTTP-EQUIVE="REFRESH" URL="HTTP://`
          `WWW.MYSITE.COM/INDEX.HTM">`

Description   The URL attribute specifies the name of the document to
          be refreshed. By default, the client will REFRESH the
          current document if a URL is not specified.

Value   URL

MULTICOL

Miscellaneous

Usage `<MULTICOL>This text will be split into two (multiple) columns by default. </MULTICOL>`

Description The MULTICOL tag renders the specified text in multiple columns.

Attributes ## COLS

Usage `<MULTICOL COLS="3">This text will be split into three (multiple) columns. </MULTICOL>`

Description The value of the COLS attribute specifies the number of columns to be used. Columns of text will fill the available viewing space.

Value Digit

GUTTER

Usage `<MULTICOL COLS="3" GUTTER="10">This text will be split into three multiple columns, separated by ten pixels of white space. </MULTICOL>`

Description The value of the GUTTER attribute specifies the amount of space between columns, in pixels. The default value is 10 pixels.

Value Pixels

WIDTH

Usage	`<MULTICOL COLS="3" WIDTH="100">This text will be split into three columns, each 100 pixels in width.</MULTICOL>`
Description	The value of the WIDTH attribute specifies the width of all columns.
Value	Pixels

NOBR

Structural Definition

Usage   `<NOBR>HTTP://WWW.MYSITE.COM</NOBR>`

Description   The NOBR tag keeps a browser from breaking a line of text.

NOFRAMES

Usage   `<NOFRAMES>This text will be displayed if frames cannot be shown.</NOFRAMES>`

Description   The NOFRAMES tag directs the browser to display alternate text should the browser be incapable of displaying frames. It is up to the HTML author to provide text content if FRAME content is not displayable.

OL

Lists

Usage
```
<OL>
<LI>This is list item uno.
<LI>This is list item dos.
</OL>
```

Description OL stands for "Ordered List." The OL tag, by default, directs the browser to number the list items inside the OL tags.

Attribute ## COMPACT

Usage
```
<OL COMPACT>
<LI>This is list item uno.
<LI>This is list item dos.
</OL>
```

Description The COMPACT attribute reduces the space between items on an ordered list.

Value —

START

Usage
```
<OL START=3>
<LI>This is list item uno.
<LI>This is list item dos.
<LI>This is list item tres.
</OL>
```

Description   The START attribute directs the browser to begin the ordered list with the specified number. This attribute allows the HTML author to split ordered lists into different groups while retaining an original number sequence.

Value   Digit

TYPE

Usage
```
<OL TYPE=A>
<LI>This is list item uno.
<LI>This is list item dos.
</OL>
```

Description   The TYPE attribute specifies the type of characters used to order an ordered list.

Acceptable character types are:

A   uppercase letters
a   lowercase letters
I   uppercase Roman numerals
i   lowercase Roman numerals
1   Digits

Value
```
A
a
I
I
Digit
```

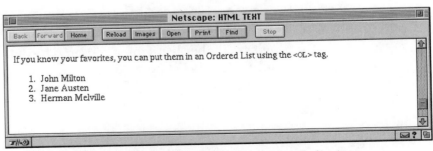

The OL tag, by default, directs the browser to number the list items.

OPTION

Forms

Usage
```
<SELECT NAME="GROUP CATEGORY">
<OPTION SELECTED>Home
<OPTION> About
<OPTION> Humor
<OPTION> What's New
</SELECT>
```

Description   Text specified with the OPTION tag is rendered as an item in a list box.

Attribute   **SELECTED**

Usage
```
<P>
<SELECT NAME="Group Category">
<OPTION SELECTED>Home
<OPTION> Coming Attractions
<OPTION> Any Other Page
<OPTION> Yet Another Page </SELECT>
</P>
```

Description   The SELECTED attribute directs the browser to display the specified SELECTED option as the default selected item in a list box.

The OPTION SELECTED will appear as highlighted text and will be sent to the server as the option *selected* unless another list item is chosen. The default OPTION SELECTED is list item number 1, unless another is specified.

Value   Text

VALUE

Usage
```
<P>
<SELECT NAME="Group Category">
<OPTION SELECTED>Home
<OPTION VALUE="1"> Page 1
<OPTION VALUE="2"> Page 2
<OPTION VALUE="3"> Page 3 </SELECT>
</P>
```

Description   The VALUE attribute specifies content to be returned to the server when the list item is selected and submitted.

Value   Text

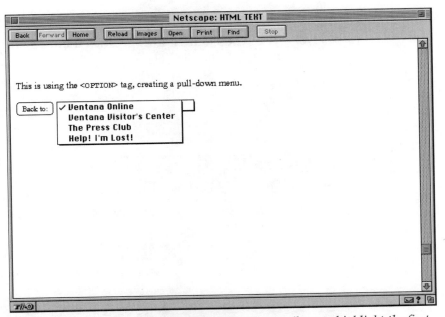

*The **OPTION** tag makes use of the **SELECTED** attribute to highlight the first item on this list.*

P

Structural Definition

Usage   `<P>This is a short paragraph. </P>`

Description   The P attribute indicates the beginning and ending of a paragraph of text.

Attribute **ALIGN**

Usage   `<P ALIGN=CENTER>This text will be centered.</P>`

Description   The ALIGN attribute specifies that text will be aligned to the LEFT, the RIGHT, or the CENTER.

Value   CENTER
LEFT
RIGHT

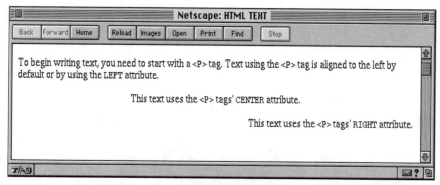

*The **P** tag can center text to the **LEFT, CENTER** or **RIGHT**. This text is rendered with the **CENTER** attribute.*

PARAM

Usage   `<PARAM NAME=MY_PARAMETER VALUE=MY_VALUE>`

Description   The PARAM tag passes additional parameters to a Java applet.

Attributes   ## NAME

Usage   `<PARAM NAME=MY_PARAMETER VALUE=MY_VALUE>`

Description   The NAME attribute specifies text used as a name for an explicit parameter.

Value   Text

VALUE

Usage   `<PARAM NAME=MY_PARAMETER VALUE=MY_VALUE>`

Description   The VALUE attribute specifies the value of the specified parameter to be passed to a Java applet.

Value   Text

PLAINTEXT

Structural Definition

Usage

```
<PLAINTEXT>This text will be rendered using a fixed-width
font!</PLAINTEXT>
```

Description

The PLAINTEXT tag directs the browser to display specified text in a plain, monospaced font without regard to other tags applied to the same text.

This tag is rendered unreliably by some browsers and is actually replaced with the PRE tag by some browsers/editors.

PRE

Structural Definition

Usage   `<PRE>The PRE tag is useful when you want a browser to display text in its original form.</PRE>`

Description   The PRE or "preformatted" tag retains spaces and line feeds in bodies of text. Many browsers display text formatted with PRE in a monospaced font.

S

Structural Definition

Usage `<S>This text will have a line drawn through its length.</S>`

Description The S tag directs the browser to draw a strike-through line upon the specified text.

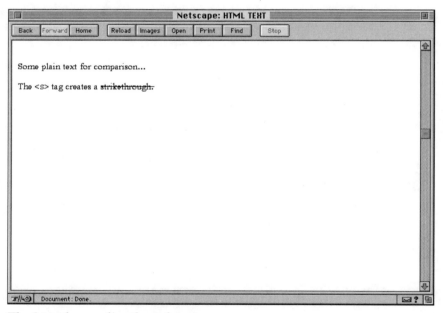

The S tag draws a line through text.

SAMP

Structural Definition

Usage   `<SAMP>This tag is useful in displaying lines of code!</SAMP>`

Description   Text specified by the SAMP tag is rendered in a monospaced font.

SCRIPT

Usage
```
<SCRIPT>
... JavaScript code ...
</SCRIPT>
```

Description The SCRIPT tag directs the browser to implement JavaScript commands enclosed.

Attributes ## LANGUAGE

Usage
```
<SCRIPT LANGUAGE="JavaScript">
... JavaScript code ...
</SCRIPT>
```

Description The value of the LANGUAGE attribute specifies the scripting language in use.

Value Text

SELECT

Forms

Usage
```
<SELECT NAME="Back to:">
<OPTION VALUE="1">Ventana Online
<OPTION VALUE="2">Ventana Visitor's Center
<OPTION VALUE="4">Help, I'm Lost!
</SELECT>
```

Description The SELECT tag directs the client browser to render a drop-down list box.

Attribute ## MULTIPLE

Usage
```
<SELECT NAME="Back to:" MULTIPLE>
<OPTION VALUE="1">Ventana Online
<OPTION VALUE="2">Ventana Visitor's Center
<OPTION VALUE="4">Help, I'm Lost!
</SELECT>
```

Description The MULTIPLE attribute allows users to select more than one item from a list box.

Value —

NAME

Usage
```
<SELECT NAME="Back to:">
<OPTION VALUE="1">Ventana Online
<OPTION VALUE="2">Ventana Visitor's Center
<OPTION VALUE="4">Help, I'm Lost!
</SELECT>
```

Description The NAME attribute creates a title used to label a list box. Text specified with the NAME tag is not displayed by the browser.

Value Text

SIZE

Usage
```
<SELECT NAME="Back to:" SIZE="1">
<OPTION VALUE="1">Ventana Online
<OPTION VALUE="2">Ventana Visitor's Center
<OPTION VALUE="4">Help, I'm Lost!
</SELECT>
```

Description The value of the SIZE attribute specifies the number of options to be made visible at all times.

Value Digit

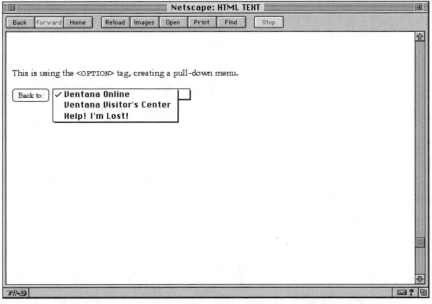

*The **SELECT** tag directs the client browser to render a drop-down list box.*

SMALL

Structural Definition

Usage   <SMALL>This text is rendered in a smaller font size.</SMALL>

Description   Text specified by the SMALL tag will be rendered in a font size smaller than the default text size.

SPACER

Usage   `<SPACER TYPE=HORIZONTAL SIZE=20>`

Description   The SPACER tag directs the client browser to render white space around specified text. This tag can create blocks of white space to flow text around.

Attributes   ## ALIGN

Usage   `<SPACER ALIGN=LEFT SIZE="20">This white space beside this text will align to the left.</SPACER>`

Description   The ALIGN attribute aligns white space to the specified value.

Value   CENTER
LEFT
RIGHT

HEIGHT

Usage   `<SPACER SIZE="20" HEIGHT-"20">This white space will be 20 pixels in height. </SPACER>`

Description   The value of the HEIGHT attribute specifies the height of the white space.

Value   Pixels

SIZE

Usage `<SPACER ALIGN=LEFT SIZE=20>This text will have 20 pixels of white space to the left of it.</SPACER>`

Description The value of the SIZE attribute specifies the width of the white space, in pixels.

Value Pixels

TYPE

Usage `<SPACER TYPE=HORZONTAL ALIGN=LEFT SIZE="20">This text will have 20 pixels of white space to the left of it.</SPACER>`

Description The value of the TYPE attribute specifies the direction in which white space is "stacked".

Value `HORIZONTAL`
`VERTICAL`

WIDTH

Usage `<SPACER ALIGN=CENTER WIDTH="200">This text will be centered in a white space 200 pixels in width.</SPACER>`

Description The value of the WIDTH attribute specifies the overall width of the white space area.

Value Pixels

STRIKE

Structural Definition

Usage `<STRIKE>This text will have a line drawn throughout its length.`
`</STRIKE>`

Description Text specified with the STRIKE tag is rendered as "lined-out" by
the browser.

STRONG

Usage   `<STRONG>This text will be rendered in BOLD.</STRONG>`

Description   Text specified with the STRONG tag is rendered in bold. Not all browsers render the STRONG tag properly, substituting italicized text instead.

SUB

Structural Definition

Usage   `<SUB>This text will be rendered in subscript fashion.</SUB>`

Description   The SUB tag directs the browser to display specified text in subscript.

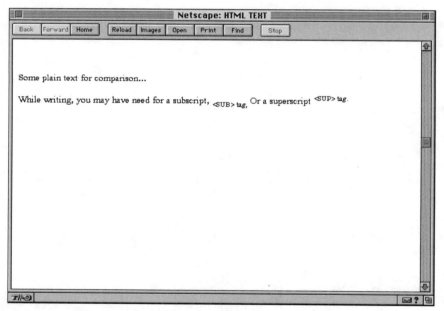

*The **SUB** tag renders text in subscript fashion.*

SUP

Structural Definition

Usage   `<SUP>This text will be rendered in superscript fashion.</SUP>`

Description   The SUP tag directs the browser to display specified text in superscript.

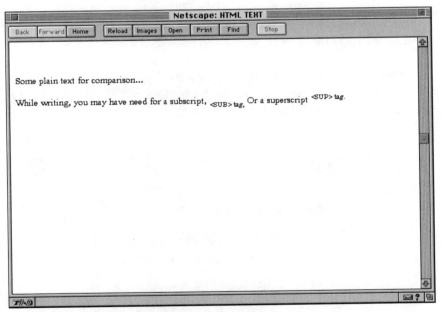

*The **SUP** tag renders text in superscript fashion.*

TABLE

Tables

Usage
```
<TABLE>
<TR>
<TH> Heading text</TH>
<TD> 1st row of text.</TD>
<TD> 2nd row of text.</TD>
<TD> 3rd row of text.</TD>
</TR>
</TABLE>
```

Description The TABLE tag specifies the beginning and the end of a table. All tags used to construct a table must be included between the TABLE tags.

Attributes ## ALIGN

Usage `<TABLE ALIGN=LEFT>`

Description The value of the ALIGN attribute directs the browser to align a table in the viewing area.

Value
```
CENTER
LEFT
RIGHT
```

BACKGROUND

Usage `<TABLE BACKGROUND="MYFILE.GIF">`

Description The BACKGROUND attribute specifies the URL of a background image, displayed behind text.

Value URL

TABLE • **115**

BGCOLOR

Usage	`<TABLE BGCOLOR="GREEN">`
Description	BGCOLOR specifies the background color of cells in a table.
Value	Color Name Hex Value RGB Value

BORDER

Usage	`<TABLE BORDER="5">`
Description	BORDER specifies the width of the table border, in pixels.
Value	Pixels

BORDERCOLOR

Usage	`<TABLE BORDERCOLOR="BLACK">`
Description	BORDERCOLOR specifies the color of a table's border.
Value	Color Name Hex Value RGB Value

BORDERCOLORDARK

Usage   `<TABLE BORDERCOLORDARK=BLUE>`

Description   The value of the BORDERCOLORDARK attribute specifies the color of the shaded edge of a 3D table border. Colors can be specified as Color Names, Hex values, or RGB values.

Value   Color Name
Hex Value
RGB Value

BORDERCOLORLIGHT

Usage   `<TABLE BORDERCOLORLIGHT="#505050>`

Description   The value of the BORDERCOLORLIGHT attribute specifies the color of the side of a 3D border that is *not* shaded. Colors can be specified as color names, RGB values, or Hex values.

Value   Color Name
Hex Value
RGB Value

CELLPADDING

Usage   `<TABLE CELLPADDING=2>`

Description   The value of the CELLPADDING attribute specifies the thickness of a cell wall in a table, in pixels.

Value   Pixels

TABLE • **117**

CELLSPACING

Usage   `<TABLE CELLSPACING=10>`

Description   The value of the CELLSPACING attribute specifies the amount of space between table cells, in pixels.

Value   Pixels

FRAME

Usage   `<TABLE FRAME="VOID">`

Description   The value of the FRAME attribute specifies the way frames appear around tables.
The list of values that can be applied with TABLE FRAME:

ABOVE	Renders a border at the top of a table frame.
BELOW	Renders a border at the bottom of a table frame.
BOX	Renders a border on all sides of a framed table.
HSIDES	Renders a border at the top and the bottom of a table frame.
LHS	Renders a border on the left side of a framed table.
RHS	Renders a border on the right side of a framed table.
VOID	Removes any existing outside borders.
VSIDES	Renders a border on the left and right sides of a framed table.

Value   ABOVE
          BELOW
          BOX
          HSIDES
          LHS
          RHS
          VOID
          VSIDES

RULES

Usage   `<TABLE RULES="ROWS">`

Description   The RULES attribute specifies how horizontal rules are used as borders within the interior of a table. The TBODY, THEAD, or TFOOT tag must be used in order to render the RULES attribute.

ALL	Renders a rule between every row and column in a table.
BASIC	Renders a rule between the TBODY, THEAD, and TFOOT segments of a table.
COLS	Renders a rule between every pair of columns in a table.
NONE	Removes any existing interior rules.
ROWS	Renders a rule between every pair of rows in a table.

Value   ALL
          BASIC
          CALLS
          NONE
          ROWS

TABLE • **119**

WIDTH

Usage `<TABLE WIDTH="60%">`

Description The WIDTH attribute specifies the width of the table in pixels or as a percentage of the viewing space displayed by the browser.

Value Pixels
%

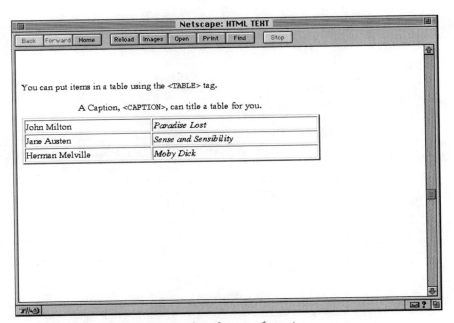

*The **TABLE** tag renders content in columnar formats.*

TD

Usage   `<TD>This text comprises the contents of a single cell.</TD>`

Description   Text enclosed in the TD (table data) tags is displayed in a single cell.

Attribute ALIGN

Usage   `<TD ALIGN=CENTER>This text will be centered in its cell.</TD>`

Description   The ALIGN attribute directs the browser to align specified text to the LEFT, the CENTER, or the RIGHT of a cell.

Value   `CENTER`
`LEFT`
`RIGHT`

COLSPAN

Usage   `<TD COLSPAN=2>This cell will span two columns.</TD>`

Description   The COLSPAN attribute allows you to make a single cell that spans the same space as a given number of cells in other rows; the number you specify indicates the number of cells adjacent and to the right that are to be combined into that single cell.

Value   Digit

NOWRAP

Usage `<TD NOWRAP>This text will be a single line within a table cell.</TD>`

Description The NOWRAP attribute prohibits the browser from wrapping text in a cell.

Value —

ROWSPAN

Usage `<TD ROWSPAN=5>This cell will span five rows.</TD>`

Description The value of the ROWSPAN attribute specifies the number of cells to be combined into a single cell. Only the cells immediately below are effected.

Value Digit

VALIGN

Usage `<TD VALIGN=TOP>This text will align to the top of the cell containing it.</TD>`

Description The value of the VALIGN or "vertical alignment" attribute directs the browser to align text to the TOP, the MIDDLE, or the BOTTOM of a cell.

Value TOP
MIDDLE
BOTTOM

WIDTH

Usage `<TD WIDTH=75%>This cell will take up 75 percent of the tables width, regardless of how large or small the borwser renders the table.</TD>`

Description The value of the WIDTH attribute determines how the browser renders the width of a cell. WIDTH values can be specified in either pixels or in a percentage of the overall table width of the table.

Value Pixels
%

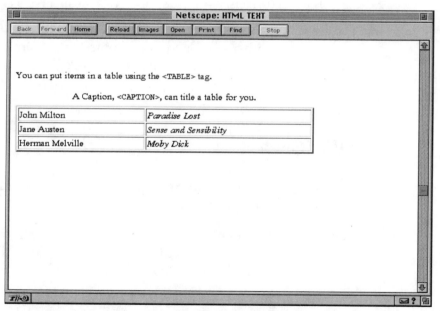

*Text rendered within a single cell is enclosed by a **TD** (table data) tag..*

TEXTAREA

Usage See attributes for examples of usage.

Description The TEXTAREA tag creates a text box for the input of data by the user. Attributes of the TEXTAREA tag tailor the configuration and functionality of the text box.

Attribute ## COLS

Usage `<TEXTAREA COLS=20>`

Description The value of the COLS attribute specifies the visible height of a text box, in characters.

Value Digit

NAME

Usage `<TEXTAREA NAME="TEXT_BOX">`

Description The value of the NAME attribute specifies a name for the input. The NAME attribute is required.

Value Text

ROWS

Usage   `<TEXTAREA ROWS=3 COLS=20>`

Description   The ROWS attribute specifies the visible width of the text box, in fixed-width characters.

Value   Digit

WRAP

Usage   `<TEXTAREA NAME="TEXT_BOX" COLS=2 ROWS=30 WRAP=VIRTUAL>`

Description   The WRAP attribute utilizes three values:

     OFF   Directs the browser to turn word wrap off (but only within the text box).

     VIRTUAL   Directs the browser to accept text in long single lines but wrap the text in the visible part of the text box.

     PHYSICAL   Directs the browser to send text exactly as it is entered by the user.

Value   OFF
          VIRTUAL
          PHYSICAL

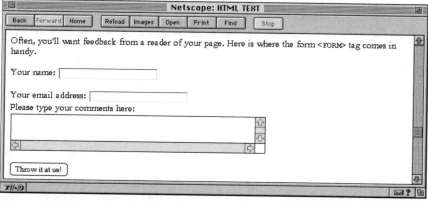

*The **TEXTAREA** tag creates a text box for the input of data by the user.*

TH

Tables

Usage   `<TH>This text is an example of a table heading. </TH>`

Description   The TH tag directs the browser to display the specified text as a table heading.

Attributes   ## ALIGN

Usage   `<TH ALIGN=LEFT>This text is aligned to the left. </TH>`

Description   The ALIGN attribute determines how text is displayed in the table header. The possible attributes are LEFT, RIGHT, and CENTER.

Value   CENTER
LEFT
RIGHT

COLSPAN

Usage   `<TH COLSPAN=9>`

Description   The value of the COLSPAN attribute determines the width of the table header, in cells. The value of COLSPAN is specified as a number of fixed-width characters.

Value   Digit

HALIGN

Usage   `<TH HALIGN=CENTER>This text is centered.</TD>`

Description   The value of the HALIGN attribute determines how table header text is aligned within its cell.

Value   CENTER
LEFT
RIGHT

NOWRAP

Usage   `<TH NOWRAP>This text will not be wrapped.</TH>`

Description   The NOWRAP attribute directs the client browser to disallow wrapping of text within a table header cell.

Value   —

ROWSPAN

Usage   `<TH ROWSPAN=5>`

Description   The value of the ROWSPAN attribute determines the number of rows to be spanned by the table header.

Value   Digits

WIDTH

Usage	`<TH WIDTH=90%>`
Description	The value of the WIDTH attribute determines how wide the table header cell will be, either in pixels or as a percentage of the width of the table.
Value	Pixels %

TBODY

Structural Definition

Usage
```
<TABLE>
<TBODY>This is the body of a table.
</TBODY>
</TABLE>
```

Description   Large HTML documents can require that lengthy tables be rendered on several "pages," especially when printed on paper. To ensure that consistent page headers and footers are correctly placed on the printed pages of long documents, page bodies, headers, and footers can be distinguished in HTML using the TBODY, THEAD, and TFOOT tags.

The TBODY tag groups table rows into an organized unit whose content is distinguished from headers and footers by a horizontal rule.

The TBODY tag is required if THEAD and TFOOT are used.

Attribute   HALIGN

Usage
```
<TABLE>
<TBODY HALIGN=CENTER>This body text will be aligned at
the center of the cell.
</TBODY>
</TABLE>
```

Description   The HALIGN attribute directs the browser to align text to the LEFT, the CENTER, or the RIGHT of a cell.

Value   CENTER
LEFT
RIGHT

VALIGN

Usage   `<TABLE>`
`<TBODY VALIGN=TOP>This text is aligned at the top.`
`</TBODY>`
`</TABLE>`

Description   The VALIGN attribute directs the browser to align text to the TOP, the MIDDLE, or the BOTTOM of a cell.

Value   `BOTTOM`
`MIDDLE`
`TOP`

TFOOT

Structural Definition

Usage
```
<TABLE>
<TFOOT>This text will appear in the footer of the document.
</TFOOT>
</TABLE>
```

Description
The TFOOT tag directs the browser to render footer information. The TFOOT tag is used primarily to render a footer on multiple pages when page devices such as printers may be in use.

Some browsers may render TBODY, THEAD, and TFOOT tags as fixed headers and footers on the screen, where only the body of the table scrolls.

Attribute **HALIGN**

Usage
```
<TABLE>
<TFOOT HALIGN=CENTER>This text is centered as a
footer.
</TFOOT>
</TABLE>
```

Description
The HALIGN attribute directs the browser to display text to the LEFT, the CENTER, or the RIGHT of the table footer.

Value
```
CENTER
LEFT
RIGHT
```

VALIGN

Usage   `<TABLE>`
`<TFOOT VALIGN=TOP>`This text is aligned at the top of a cell.
`</TFOOT>`
`</TABLE>`

Description   The VALIGN attribute directs the browser to display text to the TOP, the MIDDLE, or the BOTTOM of the table footer.

Value   `BOTTOM`
`MIDDLE`
`TOP`

THEAD

Structural Definition

Usage
```
<TABLE>
<THEAD>This text appears as a header on every page you print.
</THEAD>
</TABLE>
```

Description
The THEAD tag directs the browser to render page header information before the body of the table. The THEAD tag is used primarily to render a header on multiple pages when page devices such as printers may be in use.

Some browsers may render TBODY, THEAD, and TFOOT tags as fixed headers and footers on the screen, where only the body of the table scrolls.

Attributes

HALIGN

Usage
```
<TABLE>
<THEAD HALIGN=LEFT>This text will appear as a header
on every page you print out.
</THEAD>
</TABLE>
```

Description
The HALIGN attribute directs the browser to display text to the LEFT, the CENTER, or the RIGHT of the table header.

Value
```
CENTER
LEFT
RIGHT
```

VALIGN

Usage
```
<TABLE>
<THEAD HALIGN=LEFT>This text will appear as a header
on every page you print out.
</THEAD>
</TABLE>
```

Description
The VALIGN attribute directs the browser to display text to the TOP, the MIDDLE, or the BOTTOM of the table header.

Value
```
BOTTOM
MIDDLE
TOP
```

TITLE

Structural Definition

Usage   `<TITLE>This is my Home Page title!</TITLE>`

Description   The TITLE tag serves as the title of an HTML document, rendered on the browser's title bar. Some browsers will not render a string of text in a window title bar that is more than 64 characters in length.

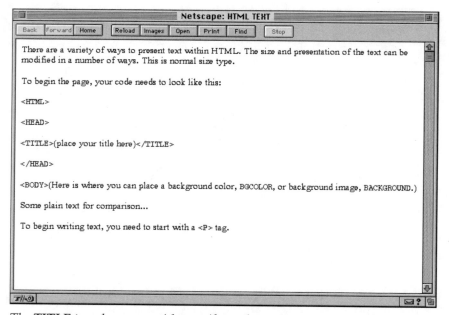

*The **TITLE** tag places your title text (for each page) on the title bar of the user's browser.*

TR

Tables

Usage
```
<TABLE>
<TR> This text appears in a single row.</TR>
</TABLE>
```

Description The TR tag directs the browser to display one or more cells inside a single row in a table.
The closing tag is not required.

Attribute ## HALIGN

Usage
```
<TR HALIGN=LEFT>This text will align to the CENTER!
</TR>
```

Description The value of the HALIGN attribute directs the browser to display text at the LEFT, the CENTER, or the RIGHT of a cell.

Value
```
CENTER
LEFT
RIGHT
```

VALIGN

Usage
```
<TR VALIGN=LEFT>This text will align to the TOP!</TR>
```

Description The value of the VALIGN attribute directs the client browser to display text at the TOP, the MIDDLE, or the BOTTOM of a cell.

Value
```
BOTTOM
MIDDLE
TOP
```

TT

Usage   `<TT>This text will be rendered in a Courier-like font.</TT>`

Description   The TT (teletype) tag directs the browser to render text in a fixed-width font to create an illusion that a teletype machine printed the displayed text. TT is synonymous with CODE in most browsers.

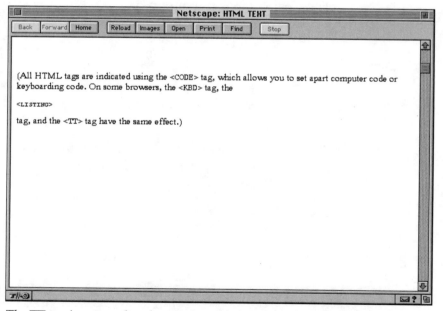

The **TT** *tag is yet another that renders text in a monospaced font to emulate teletype text.*

U

Usage   `<U>This text will be underlined by the browser.</U>`

Description   The U (underline) tag causes text to be underlined by the browser.

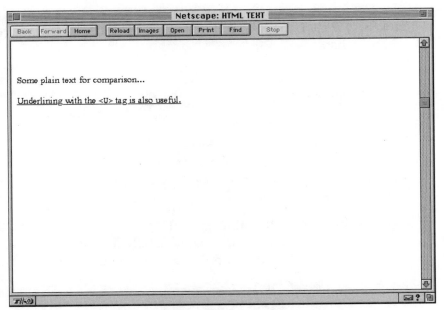

*The **U** tag directs the browser to underscore specified text.*

UL

Lists

Usage   `<UL>`
`<LI>This is the first item on the list.`
`<LI>This text is the second item on the list.`
`</UL>`

Description   The UL (unordered list) tag directs the browser to create a bulleted list.

Attribute   **TYPE**

Usage   `<UL TYPE=SQUARE>`
`<LI>This line is first on the list.`
`<LI>This line is second on the list.`
`</UL>`

Description   The value of the TYPE attribute directs the browser to substitute a DISC, a CIRCLE, or a SQUARE for the standard bullet used on an unordered list.

Value   `CIRCLE`
`DISK`
`SQUARE`

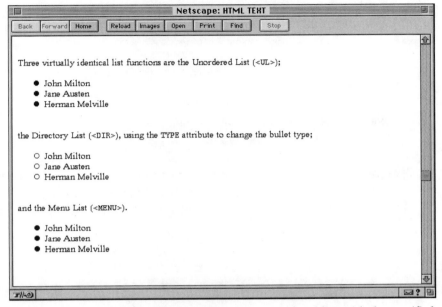

*The **UL** tag directs the browser to construct an unordered list with the specified text.*

VAR

Structural Definition

Usage   `<VAR>This text will be rendered in a fixed-width or an italicized font.</VAR>`

Description   The VAR or "variable" tag directs the browser to render text in a smaller, fixed-width font. Some HTML editors convert the VAR tag to I by default. VAR is synonymous with CODE in most browsers.

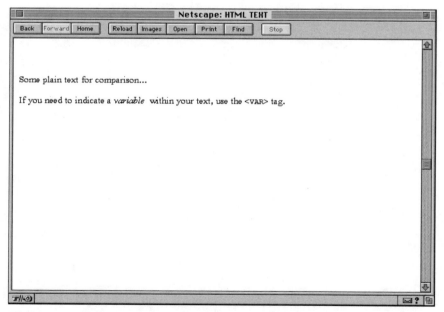

*The **VAR** tag directs the browser to render text either in a smaller, fixed-width font or as italics, as seen here.*

WBR

Structural Definition

Usage   `<WBR>This tag will force the breaking of this line of text.`
`</WBR>`

Description   The WBR or "word break" tag directs the browser to override other tags and break the line of specified text, even if other tags preclude line breaks.

The WBR tag is used primarily to manage exceptions within a block of NOBR text.

Note that widespread support for this tag is waning.

II

The JavaScript Reference

This part provides a quick reference to JavaScript objects, arrays, properties, methods, event handlers, and programming keywords. For additional reference, see the Netscape JavaScript Authoring Guide at http://home.netscape.com/eng/mozilla/3.0/handbook/javascript/index.html.

abs
Method

This Math method, Math.abs(*number*), obtains the absolute value of its argument.

acos
Method

This Math method, Math.acos(*number*), calculates the arc cosine of its argument (angle in radians whose cosine is the number).

action
Property

This form property is a string specifying a destination URL to which form data are to be submitted.

alert
Method

This window method displays a message in an Alert dialog box. No user action is required except to hit the OK button.

Example
```
<FORM>
<INPUT TYPE="button" NAME="My Button" VALUE="Click Me"
   onClick="alert('Thanks, I needed that!')">
</FORM>
```

See Also   confirm, prompt methods

alinkColor

This document property is a string specifying the color of a link over which the pointer is positioned when the mouse button is depressed. The color may be given by its name or as an RGB triplet, such as "aqua" or "00FFFF."

Examples   The following statements are equivalent:
```
document.alinkColor="aqua"
document.alinkColor="00FFFF"
```

See Also   bgColor, fgColor, linkColor, vlinkColor properties

anchor

This string method is used to create an HTML anchor that is used as a hypertext target. Use write or writeln to display the anchor so that it can be clicked to initiate loading of the target document. Anchors created with the anchor method become elements in the anchors array.

See Also   link method

anchor

An anchor object is a text string created to be the target of a hypertext link. It can be created via the anchor method or the HTML.

Property of   document object

Description   A document may contain a number of anchors, collected into an anchors array, and referenced by indexing as

```
document.anchors[0]
    document.anchors[1]
    document.anchors[2]
```

The length property, document.anchors.length, shows how many elements are in the array.

See Also   link object

appCodeName, appName, appVersion
Property

These navigator properties, navigator.appCodeName, navigator.appName, and navigator.appVersion, are strings specifying the code name, name, and version of the browser. They are read-only and can be useful in verifying that Netscape or another specific browser is being used.

See Also   userAgent property

array
Object

An array object allows collection of several items of related data under the same variable name. There is a built-in array object in Netscape Navigator 3.0, but you can define your own in earlier versions using the function statement.

Syntax   There are two types of built-in arrays: associative and ordinal. For an associative array, each index element is a string. For example,

```
houses["paint"] = "White"
    houses["wood"]  = "Cedar"
    houses["mason"] = "Brick"
```

For an ordinal array, the index elements are numbers starting with zero. For example,

```
houses[0] = "White"
  houses[1] = "Cedar"
  houses[2] = "Brick"
```

If the built-in array is not available in your browser, use a function statement to make an array of length n as follows:

```
function myArray(n) {
  this.length = n
  for (var I = 1; I <= n; I++) {
    this[I] = null;
    }
  return this
  }
```

Note that the for loop ranges from 1 to n, not 0 to $n - 1$. The 0 position is reserved for the length of the array. To create an array of houses of length 3, for example, use the following statement:

```
houses = myArray(3)
```

See Also   function statement

asin
Method

This Math method, Math.asin(*number*), calculates the arc sine of its argument (angle in radians whose sine is the number).

atan
Method

This Math method, Math.atan(*number*), calculates the arc tangent of its argument (angle in radians whose tangent is the number).

back

Method

This history method, history.back(), moves the display to the previous URL in the history list. It is the same as clicking the Back button in the Navigator toolbar.

See Also   forward, go methods

bgColor

Property

This document property, document.bgColor, is a string specifying the color of the display background. The color may be given by its name or as an RGB triplet, such as "aqua" or "00FFFF."

Examples   The following statements are equivalent:

```
document.bgColor="aqua"
document.bgColor="00FFFF"
```

See Also   fgColor, linkColor, alinkColor, vlinkColor properties

big

Method

This string method is used with the write or writeln method to display the string in a big font as if it were in an HTML BIG tag.

Examples   The big method along with the corresponding methods small and fontsize are illustrated as follows:

```
a = "JavaScript"
document.write(a.small())
document.write("<P>" + a.big())
document.write("<P>" + a.fontsize(7))
```

See Also   fontsize, small methods

blink

This string method can be used with write or writeln to cause a string to blink as if it were in an HTML BLINK tag.

Example The blink method along with corresponding methods bold, italics, and strike are illustrated as follows:

```
document.write("<P>" + "Only my eyes blink".blink())
document.write("<P>" + "Big Pine Tree".bold())
document.write("<P>" + "Lean and Mean".italics())
document.write("<P>" + "Three strikes and you're
    out".strike())
```

See Also bold, italics, strike methods

blur

The blur method is used to remove focus from an element in a form or from a password, select, text, or textarea object. It disables input to that element or object.

Method Of password, select, text, textarea

See Also focus, select methods

bold

This string method is used with write or writeln to cause a string to be displayed as bold as if it were in an HTML B tag. For example,

```
document.write("<P>" + "Big Pine Tree".bold())
```

or

```
<P><B> Big Pine Tree </B>
```

See Also blink, italics, strike methods

break

This is a programming keyword for exiting or breaking out of a loop. Program execution resumes at the next line of the script following the loop.

See also   continue (for interrupting an iteration and resuming at the top of the loop).

button

This small rectangular object is inserted into a display to enable user response to the display contents. It is an element of a form and must be defined within the FORM tag.

Syntax   The general form of a button is

```
<FORM>
<INPUT
  TYPE="button"
  NAME="buttonName"
  VALUE="buttonText"
  [onClick="handlerText"]>
</FORM>
```

Here, VALUE is the label to appear on the button face, and onClick is an optional event handler to enable recognition of a user response. Clicking on the button causes execution of the script specified by the event handler.

Property Of   form

Methods   click

Event Handlers   onClick

See Also   form, reset, submit objects

ceil

This Math method, Math.ceil(*number*), obtains the least integer greater than or equal to its argument.

See Also   floor method

charAt

This string method returns the character at index position *I* (*I* = 0 for the first character from the left, 1 for the second, and so forth). The NULL string is returned if *I* is out of range.

See Also   indexOf, lastIndexOf methods

checkbox

A checkbox object behaves as a toggle that lets the user flip it on or off. It is an element of a form and must be defined within an HTML FORM tag.

Syntax   A checkbox is defined in standard HTML syntax and contains an optional onClick event handler:

```
<FORM>
<INPUT
  TYPE="checkbox"
  NAME="checkboxName"
  VALUE="checkboxValue"
  [CHECKED]
  [onClick="handlerText"]>
  textToDisplay
</FORM>
```

Property Of | form

Properties | `checked`   the CHECKED attribute
`defaultChecked` the CHECKED attribute at load time
`name`   the NAME attribute
`value`   the VALUE attribute

Methods | click

Event Handlers | onClick

Examples | The following group of five checkboxes should all appear checked by default when initially loaded:

```
<FORM>
<B>State highest education level attained:</B>
<BR><INPUT TYPE="checkbox" NAME="Elementary School" CHECKED>
    Elementary
<BR><INPUT TYPE="checkbox" NAME="High School" CHECKED> High
    School
<BR><INPUT TYPE="checkbox" NAME="Two Year College " CHECKED>
    Junior College
<BR><INPUT TYPE="checkbox" NAME="Four Year College" CHECKED>
    College
<BR><INPUT TYPE="checkbox" NAME="Post Graduate  " CHECKED>
    Graduate
</FORM>
```

See Also | form, radio objects

checked

The checked property is a Boolean value showing the selection state of a checkbox or radio button object.

Example   If a form, myForm, and a checkbox, High_School, are defined as follows:

```
<FORM NAME="myForm">
<BR><INPUT TYPE="checkbox" NAME="High_School" CHECKED> High
    School
</FORM>
```

Then one could print the checked property by using the name of the checkbox or by using the elements array with "High_School" or 0 as index as follows:

```
document.write("<P>" + " checkbox High School " +
    document.myForm.High_School.checked)
document.write("<P>" + " checkbox[High School] " +
    document.myForm.elements["High_School"].checked)
document.write("<P>" + " checkbox[0] " +
    document.myForm.elements[0].checked)
```

See Also   defaultChecked property

clear

This document method, document.clear(), can be used to erase, or clear a document from, a window.

See Also   close, open, write, writeln methods

clearTimeout
Method

This method cancels a time-out previously set by the setTimeout method.

Syntax `clearTimeout(timeOut)`
Where timeOut identifies the time-out established by the setTimeout method.

Method Of frame, window

See Also setTimeout method

click
Method

The click method is used to simulate a mouse click within the JavaScript program. This has the same effect as an actual mouse click for button, reset, and submit; a radio button is selected for a radio; and the selection status of a checkbox is toggled on to off or off to on.

Method Ofx button, checkbox, radio, reset, submit

close
Method

With respect to a document, as document.close(), this method closes an output stream and forces residual data to be displayed.

See Also clear, open, write, writeln methods, document object

close

Method

With respect to a window, window.close() for the current window or myWindow.close() for a window named myWindow brings the window to a close (gets rid of it). This applies only to windows which have been defined by the HTML and JavaScript program, not the top one.

See Also   window object

confirm

Method

This window method places a message in a Confirm dialog box and waits for user response via the OK and Cancel buttons.

See Also   alert, prompt methods

continue

Programming Keyword

This is a programming keyword for interrupting an iteration of a loop. Program execution resumes at the top of the loop for the next iteration.

See Also   break (for exiting the loop entirely).

cookie

Property

The Navigator has a capability, quite limited for security reasons, to keep track from session to session of such things as URLs visited, in a file called cookies.txt. During any one session, this file is kept temporarily in memory as a document property, document.cookie.

See Also   hidden object

COS
Method

This Math method, Math.cos(*number*), calculates the cosine of its argument (an angle in radians).

Date
Object

The built-in Date object and its methods enable getting, setting, and manipulating dates and times.

Syntax   In the simplest case to create a Date object, today, containing today's date, one would write:

```
today = new Date()
```

In its general form, one would write:

```
someday = new Date(parameters)
```

Where someday is a JavaScript variable name for the Date object being created. The parameters for the Date constructor may be omitted as shown in the example for today's date, or they may be a string or set of integer values.

Examples   A string used to represent a date has the following form:

```
"Month day, year hours:minutes:seconds"
```

For example,

```
yearEnd = new Date("December 31, 1996 23:59:59")
```

If you omit hours, minutes, or seconds, their values will be set to zero. Following this definition of yearEnd you can use the following statements for the mm/dd/yy format:

```
dd = yearEnd.getDay()
  mm = yearEnd.getMonth() + 1
  yy = yearEnd.getYear()
```

Note that the result from getMonth() is incremented by 1. JavaScript associates 0 with January, 1 with February, and so forth. Remember this when using integers for date and time. For example,

```
yearEnd = new Date(96,11,31)
```

Methods
getDate
getDay
getHours
getMinutes
getMonth
getSeconds
getTime
getTimezoneOffset
getYear
parse
setDate
setHours
setMinutes
setMonth
setSeconds
setTime
setYear
toGMTString
toLocaleString
UTC

defaultChecked
Property

This property indicates the default selection state of a checkbox or radio button.

Property Of   checkbox, radio

See Also   checked property

defaultSelected

Property

This property of the options array indicates the default selection state of an option in a select object.

See Also index, selected, selectedIndex properties

defaultStatus

Property

This property corresponds to the message displayed in the status bar at the bottom of the window.

Property Of window

See Also status property

defaultValue

Property

The password, text, and textarea objects may be given an initial value when each object is defined. For text this is the VALUE attribute; for password it is null for security reasons; and for textarea it is taken from the HTML TEXTAREA tag. These initial values are stored as the defaultValue properties.

Property Of password, text, textarea

See Also value property

document

A document is an HTML program. The program instructs a browser or an interpreter, such as Netscape Navigator or Microsoft Internet Explorer, to build a display in one or more windows on a computer monitor. The browser begins with a document specified in its location field and may continue automatically with other documents internally referenced, ones typed into the location field, or ones selected by viewer response to program prompts or hyperlink selection.

Documents may be located in the user's computer file system, or they may reside at sites on the Internet. Local files are accessed according to their directory pathname, and Internet files are accessed according to their Universal Resource Locator (URL).

The addition of JavaScript adds client-based interactive content capabilities to an HTML program. The entries in an order form, for example, can be validated locally to reduce file transfers and corresponding delays involved in server-based validation.

JavaScript statements are interpreted along with the HTML and share with it many of the program parameters or properties of documents and windows currently loaded.

Syntax   To define a document object, use standard HTML syntax:

```
<BODY>
   BACKGROUND="backgroundImage"
   BGCOLOR="backgroundColor"
   TEXT="foregroundColor"
   LINK="unfollowedLinkColor"
   ALINK="activatedLinkColor"
   VLINK="followedLinkColor"
   [onLoad="handlerText"]
   [onUnload="handlerText"]>
</BODY>
```

BACKGROUND	the image that fills the background of the display
BGCOLOR	the background color

TEXT	the foreground color
LINK	the unfollowed link color
ALINK	the active link color
VLINK	the followed link color

Property Of window

Properties

alinkColor	the ALINK attribute
anchors	an array containing all the document anchors
bgColor	the background color
cookie	a cookie
fgColor	the TEXT attribute
forms	an array containing all the document forms
lastModified	the date the document was last modified
linkColor	the LINK attribute
links	an array contain all the document links
location	the complete URL of the document
referrer	the URL of the calling document
title	the contents of the TITLE tag
vlinkColor	the VLINK attribute

The following objects are also properties of the document object:

anchor
form
history
link

Methods clear
close
open
write
writeln

See Also frame, window objects

do while

This is a programming keyword for creating a loop to be executed at least once.

Syntax:
```
do {
    loop code
    while (conditional expression)
    }
```

See Also   for, while (programming keywords)

E

This Math property contains 2.718281828459045 for Euler's constant, the base of natural logarithms.

elements array

An array of objects in a form, this array contains an entry for each button, checkbox, hidden, password, radio, reset, select, submit, text, or textarea object that has been defined for the form.

Property Of   form

Description   You can reference elements in this array by index number or by name. If a text field, myName, and two checkboxes, cBox1 and cBox2, have been defined for myForm, these elements may be accessed by index as:

```
myForm.elements[0]
  myForm.elements[1]
    myForm.elements[2]
```

They may also be accessed by using the element's name in any of the following ways:

```
myForm.myName.value
myForm.cBox1.value
myForm.cBox2.value
```

Since this array has three elements, its length property, myForm.elements.length, would contain the number three.

See Also   form object

encoding
Property

This property of form is a string specifying the MIME encoding or encryption process to be used when the form is transmitted to the server.

Property Of   form

See Also

escape
Function

This is a built-in function to provide translation of ISO Latin-l characters to ASCII.

See Also   unescape function

eval
Function

This is a built-in function for evaluating a string. The string can be a JavaScript expression to be evaluated, or it can be one or more statements to be executed. The expression can include variables and properties of existing objects.

This function is especially useful for evaluating arithmetic expressions supplied via forms. For example, input from a form element is always a string, but a numerical value is often desired.

```
<SCRIPT>
function compute(obj) {
   obj.result.value = eval(obj.expr.value)
}
</SCRIPT>
<FORM NAME="evalform">
Enter an expression: <INPUT TYPE=text NAME="expr" SIZE=20 >
<BR>
Result: <INPUT TYPE=text NAME="result" SIZE=20 >
<BR>
<INPUT TYPE="button" VALUE="Click Me"
   onClick="compute(this.form)">
</FORM>
```

exp

Method

This Math method, Math.exp(*exponent*), calculates the value of Euler's constant raised to the exponent argument power.

See Also   log, pow methods

fgColor

Property

Text in an HTML document is considered to be foreground information, and it can be given its own color using a string literal or hexadecimal triplet, such as, document.fgColor="aqua" or document.fgColor="00FFFF." In the absence of such a specification the color set by the Navigator Options | General Preferences | Colors | Text will be used.

floor

Method

This Math method, Math.floor(*number*), obtains the largest integer less than or equal to its argument.

See Also   ceil method

focus

Method

The focus method is used to set focus on an element in a form or a password, select, text or textarea object. It enables input to that element or object by way of program statements or user keyboard input.

Method Of   password, select, text, textarea

See Also   blur, select methods

fontcolor

Method

This string method is used with write or writeln to display the string in a specified color as if it were in an HTML FONT COLOR=color tag. The color may be expressed as a hexadecimal RGB triplet or as a color name.

Example   `document.write("<P>" + "The color of water".fontcolor("aqua"))`

fontsize

Method

This string method is used with write or writeln to display the string in a big font as if it were in an HTML FONTSIZE=size tag.

Example, `document.write("<P>" + "Big Pine Tree".fontsize(7))`

See Also   big, small methods

for

Programming Keyword

This is a programming keyword for creating a loop. See also "do while" and "while."

Syntax:
```
for (initialization; conditional expression; increment) {
    loop code
    }
```

See Also   do while, while statements

form

Object (forms array)

The form object is used to collect data from the user, such as an order for goods and services, a response to a survey, or a subscription to a restricted Web site. The form provides a template that may consist of areas for entering text, making selections from lists, or simply checking items of interest. Of course, the areas, lists, and so forth may be properly annotated to give instructions. They are themselves objects of the form and are described elsewhere in this reference as checkboxes, radio buttons, selection lists, and so forth. When the form is submitted using the onSubmit event handler, it is forwarded to a server for fulfillment action.

Syntax The form object is defined in standard HTML syntax including an onSubmit event handler:

```
<FORM
    NAME="myForm"
    TARGET="myWindow"
    ACTION="serverURL"
    METHOD=GET | POST
    ENCTYPE="myMIME"
    [onSubmit="handlerText"]>
</FORM>
```

NAME	the name of the form object
TARGET	the window that form responses go to
ACTION	the URL of the server to which form field input information is sent

Property Of document

Description Elements in a form may be referenced by name or by their index position in the elements array where they are collected, one element for each INPUT tag. For example, in myForm the name of the first element or object, such as checkbox, radio, or text, is document.myForm.elements[0].name, the second, document.myForm.elements[1].name, and so forth. The number of elements in myForm is given by the elements array length property, document.myForm.elements.length.

Forms Array A document may have more than one form, although on the computer display, they will not necessarily be distinguished one from the other. See frame object to learn how to divide the display into separate viewing areas.

  When there are several forms, they may be referenced by name or by their index positions in the forms array where they are collected, one form for each FORM tag. For example, the name of the first form in a document is *document*.forms[0].name, the second *document*.forms[1].name, and so forth. The number of forms in a document is given by the forms array length property, *document*.forms.length.

Properties		
	`action`	the ACTION attribute
	`elements`	an array containing all the elements in the form
	`encoding`	the ENCTYPE attribute
	`length`	the number of elements in the form
	`name`	the name of the form
	`method`	the METHOD attribute
	`target`	the TARGET attribute

The following objects are also properties of the form object:
button
checkbox
hidden
password
radio
reset
select
submit
text
textarea

Methods   submit

Event Handlers   onsubmit

See Also   button, checkbox, hidden, password, radio, reset, select, submit, text, textarea objects

forward

Method

The forward method of the history object, history.forward (*n*), reloads the URL that is located in the history list *n*positions forward from the current one.

See Also   back, go methods

frame

Object (frames array)

A window can be divided into independent scrollable frames, each with its own boundaries and contents from its own URL. For a book, for example, a table of contents or index may be placed in a tall and narrow frame, and text from a selected title or keyword may be displayed in the remainder of the screen.

Syntax A frame object is defined in standard HTML FRAMESET and FRAME tags. The frame, which must be defined in the HEAD tag, when set shows how the window is to be divided and may include onLoad and onUnload event handlers. Each window component is then filled with its own frame information.

```
<FRAMESET
  ROWS="myRows"
  COLS="myCols"
  [onLoad="myHandler"]
  [onUnload="myHandler"]>
  [<FRAME SRC="myURL0" NAME="myFrame0">]
  [<FRAME SRC="myURL1" NAME="myFrame1">]
  ...
</FRAMESET>
```

ROWS	a comma-separated list of percentages for row division
COLS	a comma-separated list of percentages for column division
SRC	a filename or URL for frame contents
NAME	a frame name

Frames Array Frame objects can be accessed by name or by index in the frames array. This array contains an entry for each frame's FRAME tag in the frame set. For example, within the frame myFrame2, its name is given by self.name, parent.myFrame2.name, and parent.frames.name. To refer to the name of the parent window frames by index, use parent.frames[0].name for the first frame, parent.frames[1].name for the second, and so forth as follows.

```
document.write("<P>" + " myFrame2.name : " +
   parent.myFrame2.name)
document.write("<P>" + " self.name: " + self.name)
document.write("<P>" + " frames.name   : " + frames.name)
document.write("<P>" + " Number of frames at parent level: "
   + parent.frames.length)
for (var i = 0; i < parent.frames.length; i++) {
   document.write("<P>" + "Frame name[" + i + "]: " +
   parent.frames[i].name)
   }
```

Property Of   The frame object is a property of window, and the frames array is a property of both frame and window.

Methods
```
clearTimeout()
setTimeout()
```

See Also   document, window objects

function

This is a programming keyword for defining a set of code statements in the HTML HEAD to be used later in the BODY, possibly repeatedly.

Syntax:
```
function function_name [(parameters)] {
   set of code statements
   }
```

getDate

For the user defined Date object myDate, the method myDate.getDate() returns the day of the month, an integer from 1 to 31.

See Also   Date object, setDate method

getDay
Method

For the user-defined Date object myDate, the method myDate.getDay() returns the day of the week, an integer from 0 to 6, 0 for Sunday, 1 for Monday, and so forth.

See Also   Date object

getHours
Method

For the user-defined Date object myDate, the method myDate.getHours() returns the hour of the day, an integer from 0 to 23.

See Also   Date object, setHours method

getMinutes
Method

For the user-defined Date object myDate, the method myDate.getMinutes() returns the minutes of the hour, an integer from 0 to 59.

See Also   Date object, setMinutes method

getMonth
Method

For the user-defined Date object myDate, the method myDate.getMonth() returns the month of the year, an integer from 0 to 11, 0 for January, 1 for February, and so forth.

See Also   Date object, setMonth method

getSeconds
Method

For the user-defined Date object myDate, the method
myDate.getSeconds() returns the seconds of the minute, an integer
from 0 to 59.

See Also   Date object, setSeconds method

getTime
Method

For the user-defined Date object myDate, the method
myDate.getTime() returns the amount of time in milliseconds
since 1 January 1970 00:00:00.

See Also   Date object, setTime method

getTimezoneOffset
Method

For the user-defined Date object myDate, the method
myDate.getTimezoneOffset() returns the difference between local
time and GMT in minutes. This offset changes with Daylight
Savings Time changes.

See Also   Date object, toGMTString, toLocaleString methods

getYear
Method

For the user-defined Date object myDate, the method
myDate.getYear() returns the year, a two-digit number representing the actual year less 1900. You get to reprogram your
JavaScripts in 2000!

See Also   Date object, setYear method

go

Method

The go method of the history object, history.go(argument), reloads a URL according to the argument. If the argument is an integer, *delta,* then the URL reloaded is the one that is located in the history list *delta* positions from the current. Thus history.go(–1) reloads the previous URL. The value of *delta* may be negative to go backward in the history list, positive to go forward, or zero to reload the current URL. If the argument is a string, then it specifies the URL to be reloaded.

See Also back, forward methods

hash

Property

The hash property, links[*index*].hash or location.hash, is a string beginning with a hash mark (#) that specifies an anchor name in the URL.

See Also host, hostname, href, pathname, port, protocol, search properties

hidden

Object

A text object that is not displayed, a hidden object is used for passing name/value pairs when a form is submitted.

Syntax To define a hidden object:

```
<INPUT
   TYPE="hidden"
   NAME="hiddenName"
   [VALUE="textValue"]>
```

NAME="hiddenName"   specifies the name of the hidden object.
VALUE="textValue"   specifies the initial value of the hidden
                     object.

To use a hidden object's properties:

1. `hiddenName.propertyName`
2. `formName.elements[index].propertyName`

`hiddenName`	the value of the NAME attribute of a hidden object.
`formName`	either the value of the NAME attribute of a form object or an element in the forms array.
`index`	an integer representing a hidden object on a form.
	propertyName is one of the properties listed.

Property Of form

Description A hidden object is a form element and must be defined within a FORM tag.

A hidden object cannot be seen or modified by a user, but you can change the value of the object by changing its value property. You can use hidden objects for client/server communication.

Properties
`name` reflects the NAME attribute.
`value` reflects the current value of the hidden object.

Example The following example uses a hidden object to store the value of the last object the user clicked. The form contains a "Display hidden value" button that the user can click to display the value of the hidden object in an Alert dialog box.

```
<HTML>
<HEAD>
<TITLE>Hidden object example</TITLE>
</HEAD>
<BODY>
<B>Click some of these objects, then click the "Display
  value" button
<BR>to see the value of the last object clicked.</B>
<FORM NAME="form1">
<INPUT TYPE="hidden" NAME="hiddenObject" VALUE="None">
<P>
```

```
<INPUT TYPE="button" VALUE="Click me" NAME="button1"
  onClick="document.form1.hiddenObject.value=this.value">
<P>
<INPUT TYPE="radio" NAME="musicChoice" VALUE="soul-and-r&b"
  onClick="document.form1.hiddenObject.value=this.value">
  Soul and R&B
<INPUT TYPE="radio" NAME="musicChoice" VALUE="jazz"
  onClick="document.form1.hiddenObject.value=this.value">
  Jazz
<INPUT TYPE="radio" NAME="musicChoice" VALUE="classical"
  onClick="document.form1.hiddenObject.value=this.value">
  Classical
<P>
<SELECT NAME="music_type_single"
  onFocus="document.form1.hiddenObject.value=this.options
  [this.selectedIndex].text">
  <OPTION SELECTED> Red <OPTION> Orange <OPTION> Yellow
</SELECT>
<P><INPUT TYPE="button" VALUE="Display hidden value"
  NAME="button2"
  onClick="alert('Last object clicked: ' +
  document.form1.hiddenObject.value)">
</FORM>
</BODY>
</HTML>
```

See Also   cookie property

history

Object

The history object contains information on the URLs visited during a Navigator session. This information is stored in a history list that is accessible through the Navigator's Go or Window | History menu using your mouse or keyboard. Items in this list are not accessible to a JavaScript program except as the target of a history method, back, forward, and go.

Syntax   To use a history object:

1. `history.propertyName`
2. `history.methodName(parameters)`

propertyName is one of the properties listed.
methodName is one of the methods listed.

Property Of   document

Description   The history object is a linked list of URLs the user has visited, as shown in the Navigator's Go menu.

Properties   length reflects the number of entries in the history object.

Methods   `back`
`forward`
`go`

Examples   Example 1. The following example goes to the URL visited three clicks ago in the current window:

```
history.go(-3)
```

Example 2. You can use the history object with a specific window or frame. The following example causes window2 to go back one item:

```
window2.history.back()
```

Example 3. The following example causes the second frame in a frameset to go back one item:

```
parent.frames[1].history.back()
```

See Also   location object

host
Property

The host property, links[*index*].host or location.host, is a string containing the concatenation of the hostname and port properties of the URL, separated by a colon.

See Also   hash, hostname, href, pathname, port, protocol, search properties

hostname
Property

The hostname property, links[*index*].hostname or location.hostname, is a string containing the host and domain name, or IP address, of a network host (server).

See Also   hash, host, href, pathname, port, protocol, search properties

href
Property

The href property, links[*index*].href or location.href, is a string containing an entire URL.

See Also   hash, host, hostname, pathname, port, protocol, search properties

if
Programming Keyword

This is a programming keyword indicating that a set of code statements is to be executed after it is determined that a logical expression evaluates to true.

Syntax:
```
if (logical expression is true) {
    set of code statements
    }
```

if ... else
Programming Keyword

This is a programming keyword indicating that a set of code keywords must be executed after it is determined that a logical expression evaluates to true and that another set of code keywords must be executed otherwise.

Syntax:
```
if (logical expression is true) {
    set of code statements for true
    } else {
        set of code statements for false
    }
```

index
Property

This select options array property, mySelect.options[*argument*].index, is an integer containing the index of the option located in the options array at the argument position.

See Also   defaultSelected, selected, selectedIndex properties

indexOf
Method

This is a method for locating a sub-string in a string object and returning the index position of the sub-string, reading from left to right. For example, the following statement yields 5, the position (starting with zero) of the "O" in "indexOf."

```
A = "indexOf".indexOf("O")
```

isNaN

This is a built-in function, isNaN(*argument*), that returns true on UNIX platforms if the argument is not a number (NaN) and false if it is a number. On other platforms one should use parseFloat(*argument* [,*radix*]) or parseInt(*argument* [,*radix*]), which will return NaN if the argument is not a number. Otherwise, they will return the number, float or integer, parsed according to the base radix.

See Also   parseFloat, parseInt functions

italics

This string method is used with write or writeln to causes a string to be displayed in italics as if it were in an HTML I tag.

Example   `document.write("<P>" + "Lean and Mean".italics())`

or

`<P><I> Lean and Mean </I>`

See Also   blink, bold, strike methods

lastIndexOf

This is a method for locating a sub-string in a string object and returning the index position of the last such sub-string, reading from left to right. For example, the following statement yields 13, the position (starting with zero) of the last "e" in "lastIndexOf method."

```
A = "lastIndexOf method".lastIndexOf("e")
```

length

Length is a property of several different objects and properties and has the general format object.length or property.length. It is used for multiple objects and properties and contains an integer to keep up with how many are defined.

Syntax		
`anchors.length`	the number of anchors in the anchors array
`elements.length`	the number of elements in the elements array
`forms.length`	the number of forms in the forms array
`history.length`	the number of locations in the history object
`links.length`	the number of links in the links array
`myForm.length`	the number of elements in myForm
`myFrame.frames.length`	the number of frames in the frames array of myFrame
`myFrame.length`	the number of frames in myFrame
`myRadio.length`	the number of radio buttons in myRadio
`mySelect.length`	the number of options in mySelect
`mySelect.options.length`	the number of options in the options array of mySelect
`myString.length`	the number of characters in myString
`myWindow.frames.length`	the number of frames in the frames array of myWindow
`myWindow.length`	the number of frames in myWindow

Property Of frame, history, radio, select, string, window objects
anchors, elements, forms, frames, links, options arrays

linkColor

Property

This document property, document.linkColor, is a string specifying the color of its hyperlinks. The color may be given by its name or as an RGB triplet, such as "aqua" or "00FFFF," respectively.

Examples   The following statements are equivalent:

```
document.linkColor="aqua"
document.linkColor="00FFFF"
```

See Also   alinkColor, bgColor, fgColor, vlinkColor properties

link

Method

Use the link method, myString.link(URL), to create an HTML hypertext link (typically text highlighted with a different color given by document.linkColor) and associated location (URL). When the highlighted text is clicked on, the browser will attempt to get and load the document at the URL. The links array automatically collects links established with this method. Shown here is a coding example first in JavaScript:

```
document.write("Click to visit " + "Ventana".link("HTTP://
    www.vmedia.com"))
```

and then in HTML:

```
Click to visit <A HREF="http://www.vmedia.com">Ventana</A>
```

See Also   alinkColor property, anchor method

link

Object (links array)

Hypertext links created by the link method, myString.link(URL), or by HREF definitions (anchors) in HTML are considered link objects and are collected in the links array. They are synonymous with location objects and have the same properties, href, hostname, pathname, and so forth as location objects. The following code illustrates creating a link first in HTML:

```
Click to visit <A HREF="http://www.vmedia.com">Ventana</A>
```

and then by using the link method:

```
document.write("<P>" + "Click to visit :" +
    "Ventana".link("HTTP://www.vmedia.com"))
```

links array

No matter how the links are created, as given by

```
document.links.length
```

they can be printed as members of the links array:

```
for (I = 0; I <= document.links.length; I++) {
    document.write("<P>" + "links.[" + I + "]: " +
    document.links[I])
    }
```

Property Of document

Event Handlers onclick
onmouseover

See Also anchor object, link method

Literals

Fixed values are represented as literals in JavaScript. Examples include: 42 (an integer), 3.14159 (a floating-point number), and "To be or not to be" (a string).

Integer literals can be expressed in decimal (base 10, without leading zero), hexadecimal (base 16, with leading zero and x or X, 0x or 0X), or octal (base 8, with leading zero) format. Hexadecimal integers can include digits (0–9) and the letters a–f and A–F. Octal integers can include only the digits 0–7.

A floating-point literal can have the following parts: a decimal integer, a decimal point ("."), a fraction (another decimal number), an exponent, and a type suffix. The exponent part is an "e" or "E" followed by an integer, which can be signed (preceded by a "+" or "–"). A floating-point literal must have at least one digit, plus either a decimal point or "e" (or "E"). Some examples include 3.1415, –3.1E12, .1e12, and 2E–12.

A Boolean literals has one of two values: true or false.

A string literal is zero or more characters enclosed in a pair of double (") or single (') quotes, such as "blah" or 'blah' or "one line \n another line"—which illustrates use of a special character ("\n") for dividing text into two lines. Other special characters include "\b" for a backspace, "\f" for a form feed (new page), and "\t" for a tab character.

LN2 Property

This Math property contains .6931471805599453 for the natural logarithm of two.

LN10 Property

This Math property contains 2.302585092994046 for the natural logarithm of ten.

location

Object

The location object is a window property, window.location, that contains the complete URL of the current document. On initial load, this property is the same as shown in the browser location or netsite field and is the same as the location property of the document that is loaded. You cannot change the document.location in your program, but you can change window.location. Assigning a new URL to window.location causes the document from that URL to be loaded.

Syntax The location object or complete URL has the general format

```
protocol//hostname:port pathname search hash
```

whose components are described in the following properties list.

Property Of window

Properties

hash	an anchor name in the URL
host	the hostname:port portion of the URL
hostname	the host and domain name, or IP address, of a network host
href	the entire URL
pathname	the target computer (server) path portion of the URL
port	the communications port on the server
protocol	the file transmission type—HTTP, FTP, and so forth
search	a query

Examples To set the URL of the current window to the NetscapePress home page and go to that page one would write

```
window.location="http://www.netscapepress.com"
```

See Also history object, location property

location
Property

This document property, document.location, contains the complete URL of the current document. On initial load this property is the same as shown in the browser location or netsite field. It may be changed only by loading another document.

See Also   location object

log
Method

This Math method, Math.log(*number*) calculates the natural (base e) logarithm of the argument, a positive number.

LOG2E
Property

This Math property contains 1.4426950408889634 for the natural logarithm of Euler's number (E).

LOG10E
Property

This Math property contains .4342944819032518 for the base 10 logarithm of Euler's number (E).

Math
Object

The built-in Math object has properties and methods for mathematical constants and functions. For example, the Math object's PI property has the value of pi.

Syntax   A math property is accessed in an application as

```
v = Math.PI
```

To access a function, such as the trigonometric function sine, one would write

```
v = Math.sin(1.56)
```

All trigonometric methods of math take arguments in radians. It is often convenient to use the "with" statement when a section of code uses several Math constants and methods. For example,

```
with (Math) {
   a = PI * r*r
   y = r*sin(theta)
   x = r*cos(theta)
   }
```

Properties   E
             LN2
             LN10
             LOG2E
             LOG10E
             PI
             SQRT1_2
             SQRT2

Methods   abs( )   sin( )
          acos( )   sqrt( )
          asin( )   tan( )
          atan( )
          ceil( )
          cos( )
          exp( )
          floor( )
          log( )
          max( )
          min( )
          pow( )
          random( )
          round( )

max
Method

This Math method, Math.max(*number1*,*number2*), obtains the larger of the two arguments.

See Also   min method

method
Property

The method property of a form specifies how field information in the form is to be sent to the server. It is set in the <FORM> tag as the METHOD attribute to either "get" or "post".

min
Method

This Math method, Math.min(*number1*,*number2*), obtains the lesser of the two arguments.

See Also   max method

navigator
Object

This object contains information about the version of Navigator in use.

Syntax   To use a navigator object:

```
navigator.propertyName
```

where propertyName is one of the properties listed.

Description   Use the navigator object to determine the version of the Navigator being used.

Properties	appCodeName	the code name of the browser
	appName	the name of the browser
	appVersion	version information for the Navigator
	userAgent	the user-agent header

See Also   link, anchors objects

new

This is a programming keyword used in creating an object from a JavaScript prototype or constructor. To create a Date object, today, representing today's date, for example, one would write:

```
today = new Date()
```

onBlur

The onBlur event handler executes JavaScript code when a blur event occurs. A blur event occurs when a select, text, or textarea field on a form loses focus.

Event Handler Of   select, text, textarea

Example   In the following example, userName is a required text field. When a user attempts to leave the field, the onBlur event handler calls the required() function to confirm that userName has a legal value.

```
<INPUT TYPE="text" VALUE="" NAME="userName"
  onBlur="required(this.value)">
```

See Also   onChange, onFocus event handlers

onChange

The onChange event handler executes JavaScript code when a change event occurs. A change event occurs when a select, text, or textarea field loses focus and its value has been modified.

Event Handler Of select, text, textarea

Example In the following example, userName is a text field. When a user attempts to leave the field, the onBlur event handler calls the checkValue() function to confirm that userName has a legal value.

```
<INPUT TYPE="text" VALUE="" NAME="userName"
  onBlur="checkValue(this.value)">
```

See Also onBlur, onFocus event handlers

onClick

The onClick event handler executes JavaScript code when a click event occurs, that is, when an object on a form is clicked.

Event Handler Of button, checkbox, radio, link, reset, submit

Example Suppose you have created a JavaScript function called compute(). You can execute the compute() function when the user clicks a button by calling the function in the onClick event handler, as follows:

```
<INPUT TYPE="button" VALUE="Calculate"
  onClick="compute(this.form)">
```

The keyword "this" refers to the current object; in this case, the Calculate button. The construct this.form refers to the form containing the button.

onFocus

The onFocus event handler executes JavaScript code when a focus event occurs, that is, when a field receives input focus because the user has tabbed with the keyboard or clicked with the mouse.

Event Handler Of   select, text, textarea

Example   The following example uses an onFocus handler in the valueField textarea object to call the valueCheck() function.

```
<INPUT TYPE="textarea" VALUE="" NAME="valueField"
    onFocus="valueCheck()">
```

See Also   onBlur, onChange event handlers

onLoad

The onLoad event handler executes JavaScript code when a load event occurs, that is, when Navigator finishes loading a window or all frames within a FRAMESET.

Event Handler Of   window

Example   In the following example, the onLoad event handler displays a greeting message after a Web page is loaded:

```
<BODY onLoad="window.alert("Welcome to the Brave New World
    home page!")>
```

See Also   onUnload event handler

onMouseOver

Event Handler

The onMouseOver event handler executes JavaScript code when a mouseOver event occurs. A mouseOver event occurs once each time the mouse pointer moves over an object from outside that object.

Event Handler Of   link

Example   By default, the HREF value of an anchor displays in the status bar at the bottom of the Navigator when a user places the mouse pointer over the anchor. In the following example, the onMouseOver event handler provides the custom message "Click this if you dare!"

```
<A HREF="http://home.netscape.com/"
  onMouseOver="window.status='Click this if you dare!';
  return true">
  Click me</A>
```

onSelect

Event Handler

The onSelect event handler executes JavaScript code when a select event occurs, that is, when a user selects some of the text within a text or textarea field.

Event Handler Of   text, textarea

Example   The following example uses an onSelect handler in the valueField text object to call the selectState() function:

```
<INPUT TYPE="text" VALUE="" NAME="valueField"
  onSelect="selectState()">
```

onSubmit

The onSubmit event handler executes JavaScript code when a submit event occurs, that is, when a user submits a form.

Event Handler Of   form

Example   In the following example, the onSubmit event handler calls the formData() function to evaluate the data being submitted. If the data are valid, the form is submitted; otherwise, the form is not submitted.

```
form.onSubmit="return formData(this)"
```

See Also   submit object, submit method

onUnload

The onUnload event handler executes JavaScript code when an unload event occurs. An unload event occurs when you exit a document.

Event Handler Of   window

Example   In the following example, the onUnload event handler calls the cleanUp() function to perform some shutdown processing when the user exits a Web page:

```
<BODY onUnload="cleanUp()">
```

See Also   onLoad event handler

open
Method (document object)

This document method opens a stream to collect write or writeln outputs.

open
Method (window object)

This method can be used to open a new web browser window within the JavaScript program similar to using the File | New Web Browser selections from the display.

parent
Property

When a set of frames has been created, using the FRAMESET tag, and your program has transferred to one of the frames in the set, you can refer back to the calling level using the parent property. For example, the name of the calling window or frame is parent.name.

parse
Method

This is a Date method, Date.parse(*string*), which converts its argument string representing a date into the number of milliseconds since January 1, 1970, 00:00:00 local time. The date string may be in the IETF standard format, such as "Tue, 31 Dec 1996 13:30:00 GMT," or in the less formal "Dec 31, 1996"

See Also   Date object, UTC method

parseFloat, parseInt
Function

These are built-in functions for converting a string to a numeric value. ParseFloat attempts to return a floating-point number. If it encounters a character other than a sign (+ or –), a numeral (0–9), a decimal point, or an exponent, then it returns the value up to that point and ignores that character and all succeeding characters. If the first character cannot be converted to a number, it returns NaN (not a number).

The parseInt function parses its first argument, a string, and attempts to return an integer of the specified radix (base). For example, a radix of 10 instructs the function to convert its argument to a decimal number, 8, octal, 16, hexadecimal, and so on. For radixes above 10, the letters of the alphabet indicate numerals greater than 9. For example, for hexadecimal numbers (base 16), A through F are used.

If parseInt encounters a character that is not a numeral in the specified radix, it ignores it and all succeeding characters and returns the integer value parsed up to that point. If the first character cannot be converted to a number in the specified radix, it returns NaN. ParseInt truncates numbers to integer values.

password
Object

The password object is an HTML INPUT input field of type "password" on a form with the special handling feature that hides its contents on the computer screen by displaying asterisks (*), one for each character in the password.

Syntax   A password object is defined in standard HTML:

```
<INPUT
   TYPE="password" NAME="passwordName"[VALUE="textValue"]
   SIZE=integer>
```

TYPE	the password
NAME	the name of the password object
VALUE	the initial value
SIZE	the number of characters the password display field can hold without scrolling

Properties

defaultValue null;	the initial VALUE attribute is ignored
name	the NAME attribute
value	the current VALUE attribute

Methods

focus
blur
select

See Also form, text objects

pathname
Property

The pathname property, links[*index*].pathname or location.pathname, is a string containing the directory and filename for the document on the target computer (server). If the URL is for a document in a user directory on the client computer, then this property will be essentially the local directory and filename for the document.

See Also hash, host, hostname, href, pathname, port, protocol, search properties

PI
Property

This Math property contains 3.141592653589793 for pi, the number of radians in half a circle.

port

The port property, links[*index*].port or location.port, is a string containing the communications port to be used by the server for this URL. The port is often omitted for a default of 80.

See Also   hash, host, hostname, href, pathname, protocol, search properties

pow

This Math method, Math.pow(*base,exponent*), calculates the value of the base argument raised to the exponent argument power.

See Also   exp, log methods

prompt

Use this window method to display a Prompt dialog box with a message and an input field. The message provides clues as to what is being requested, and the input field provides space for a response. Both numeric and text input is allowed, and an initial or default value for the input may be included in the box. For example, the following box asks how you feel and provides for a response of "fine."

```
prompt("How do you feel?, "fine")
```

protocol

The protocol property, links[*index*].protocol or location.protocol, is a string containing the communications method, HTTP, FTP, and so forth, for transferring the file specified by the URL from a server to a client computer. If the URL is for a document in a user directory on the client computer, then the protocol will be "file:"

See Also   hash, host, hostname, href, pathname, port, search properties

radio

A radio button is an object of a form and may be clicked to indicate a user choice. The form will typically have a number of buttons for multiple choices.

Syntax   Each radio button in a form is defined in a standard HTML INPUT tag and may include an onClick event handler:

```
<FORM>
<INPUT
   TYPE="radio"
   NAME="myRadio"
   VALUE="buttonValue"
   [CHECKED]
   [onClick="myHandler"]>
   textToDisplay
<INPUT
...
</FORM>
```

NAME	the name of the radio object
VALUE	the value sent to server when the button is selected and the form is submitted
CHECKED	an indication that the button is selected
TextToDisplay	the label to display beside the button

Property Of   form

Description   A set of radio buttons may be given a single name. Individual buttons in the set may then be accessed by index. For example, the name of the first radio in the set myRadio on myForms is given by document.myForms.myRadio[0].name; the name of the second is document.myForms.myRadio[1].name; and so forth.

Properties   `checked`   an indicator of the checked condition
`defaultChecked`   the CHECKED attribute
`length`   the number of radio buttons in a set
`name`   the NAME attribute
`value`   the VALUE attribute

Methods   click

Event Handlers   onclick

See Also   checkbox, form, select objects

random
Method

This Math method, Math.random(), calculates a pseudorandom number between zero and one on UNIX platforms only.

referrer
Property

This document property contains the URL of the calling document when a user clicks a link and reaches a called document. The property, document.referrer, has meaning only in the called document.

reset

This is a reset button on an HTML form for returning all elements to their defaults.

Syntax To define a reset button, use standard HTML syntax and the onClick event handler:

```
<INPUT
  TYPE="reset"
  NAME="resetName"
  VALUE="buttonText"
  [onClick="handlerText"]>
```

NAME="resetName"   specifies the name of the reset object.

VALUE="buttonText"   specifies the text to display on the button face.

To use a reset object's properties and methods:

1. `resetName.propertyName`

2. `resetName.methodName(parameters)`

3. `formName.elements[index].propertyName`

4. `formName.elements[index].methodName(parameters)`

resetName   the value of the NAME attribute of a reset object.

formName   either the value of the NAME attribute of a form object or an element in the forms array.

index   an integer representing a reset object on a form.

propertyName   one of the properties listed.

methodName   one of the methods listed.

Property Of form

Description A reset object is a form element and must be defined within a FORM tag.

The reset button's onClick event handler cannot prevent a form from being reset; once the button is clicked, the reset cannot be canceled.

Properties   name
value

Methods   click

Event Handlers   onclick

Example   The following example displays a text object with the default value "CA" and a reset button with the text "Clear Form" displayed on its face. If the user types a state abbreviation in the text object and then clicks the Clear Form button, the original value of "CA" is restored.

```
<B>State: </B><INPUT TYPE="text" NAME="state" VALUE="CA"
  SIZE="2">
<P><INPUT TYPE="reset" VALUE="Clear Form">
```

See Also   button, form, submit objects

return
Programming Keyword

This is a programming keyword used in functions to pass a value back to the calling script.

round
Method

This Math method, Math.round(*number*), rounds the argument to its nearest integer.

search
Property

The search property, links[*index*].search or location.search, is a string beginning with a question mark (?) that specifies a query request in the URL.

See Also   hash, host, hostname, href, pathname, port, protocol properties

select
Method

The select method is used to highlight an element in a form or a password, select, text, or textarea object. It draws user attention to the element or object. One would typically use this method in conjunction with focus, which enables input.

Method Of   password, select, text, textarea objects

See Also   blur, focus methods

select
Object (options array)

A select object is a list from which one can choose a single entry. A short list is presented in its entirety, and a long list is presented in part with a scroll bar for viewing the remainder. This object is defined within the HTML SELECT tag, which in turn is defined within FORM and is thus a form element or property. Tie-in with JavaScript code is accomplished via the addition of onBlur, onChange, and onFocus event handlers.

Properties
length   the number of options in a select object
name   the name of the select object
options   the collection of entries in the OPTION tags
selectedIndex   the index of the selected option

The Options Array	The options array contains the entries in the OPTION tag of the select object. They can be accessed as mySelect.options[0], mySelect.options[2], and so forth, for the select object named mySelect. selectName is either the value of the NAME attribute of a select object or an element in the elements array.

Properties	defaultSelected	the SELECTED attribute
	index	the index of option
	length	the number of options in a select object
	name	the name of the option
	selected	enables option selection by program statement
	selectedIndex	the index of the selected option
	text	textToDisplay from the OPTION tag
	value	the value of the option

Methods	blur
	focus

Event Handlers	onBlur
	onChange
	onFocus

See Also	form, radio objects

selected

Property

This is a select object property containing a Boolean value specifying the current selection state of an option, that is, showing whether is has been selected or not.

selectedIndex
Property

This select or select options array property,
mySelect.selectedIndex, or, as is recommended,
mySelect.options.selectedIndex, is an integer containing the index
of a selected option.

See Also   defaultSelected, index, selected properties

setDate
Method

For the user-defined Date object myDate, the method
myDate.setDate(*day*) sets the day-of-the-month component of
myDate to the input argument.

See Also   Date object, getDate method

setHours
Method

For the user-defined Date object myDate, the method
myDate.setHours(*hours*) sets the hours-of-the-day component of
myDate to the input argument.

See Also   Date object, getHours method

setMinutes
Method

For the user-defined Date object myDate, the method
myDate.setMinutes(*minutes*) sets the minutes component of
myDate to the input argument.

See Also   Date object, getMinutes method

setMonth
Method

For the user-defined Date object myDate, the method myDate.setMonth(*month*) sets the month component of myDate to the input argument.

See Also   Date object, getMonth method

setSeconds
Method

For the user-defined Date object myDate, the method myDate.setSeconds(*seconds*) sets the seconds component of myDate to the input argument.

See Also   Date object, getSeconds method

setTime
Method

For the user-defined Date object myDate, the method myDate.setTime(*time*) sets the value of myDate to the input argument, the number of milliseconds since 1 January 1970 00:00:00.

See Also   Date object, getTime method

setTimeout
Method

The setTimeout method starts a time clock and performs an action or evaluates an expression after a specified delay in milliseconds has elapsed. For example, the following statement starts a time clock, timerOne, and performs a command given by "cmd" after a delay of 100 milliseconds.

```
timerONE=window.setTimeout(cmd,100)
```

setYear

Method

For the user-defined Date object myDate, the method myDate.setYear(*year*) sets the year component of myDate to the input argument.

See Also   Date object, getYear method

sin

Method

This Math method, Math.sin(*number*), calculates the sine of its argument (an angle in radians).

small

Method

This string method is used with write or writeln to display the string in a small font as if it were in an HTML FONTSIZE=small tag. For example,

```
document.write("<P>" + "Think small".small)
```

See Also   big, fontsize methods

SQRT1_2

Property

This Math property contains .7071067811865476 for the reciprocal of the square root of two.

SQRT2
Property

This Math property contains 1.4142135623730951 for the square root of two.

status
Property

This window property contains the contents of the status bar.

strike
Method

This string method is used with write or writeln to cause a string to be displayed with strikes as if it were in an HTML STRIKE tag.

Example
```
document.write("<P>" + "Three strikes and you're out".strike())
or
<P><STRIKE> Three strikes and you're out </STRIKE>
```

See Also   blink, bold, italics methods

string
Object

This is a built-in object. Whenever you assign a string value to a variable or a property, you create a string object. String literals are also string objects. For example, the statement

```
mystring = "Hello, World!"
```

creates a string object called mystring with the length or number of characters 13.

Syntax   To use a string object:

1. `stringName.propertyName`
2. `stringName.methodName(parameters)`

`stringName`	the name of a string variable.
`propertyName`	one of the string properties.
`methodName`	one of the string methods

Properties   length

Methods
anchor
big
blink
bold
charAt
fixed
fontcolor
fontsize
indexOf
italics
lastIndexOf
link
small
strike
sub
substring
sup
toLowerCase
toUpperCase

Examples   The following statement creates a string variable:

```
var last_name = "Schaefer"
```

The following statements evaluate to 8, "SCHAEFER," and "schaefer":

```
last_name.length
  last_name.toUpperCase()
  last_name.toLowerCase()
```

See Also   text, textarea objects

submit

Method

This method submits a form from client to server.

Syntax
```
formName.submit()
```
formName is the name of a form or an element in the forms array.

Method Of form

Description Use the submit method to send data in a form from a client computer to an HTTP server.

Example The following example submits a form called musicChoice:

```
document.musicChoice.submit()
```

If musicChoice is the first form created, you also can submit it with

```
document.forms[0].submit()
```

See Also submit object, onSubmit event handler

submit

Object

This is a submit button on an HTML form.

Syntax To define a submit button, use standard HTML syntax with the onClick event handler:

```
<INPUT
  TYPE="submit"
  NAME="submitName"
  VALUE="buttonText"
  [onClick="handlerText"]>
```

NAME="submitName" specifies the name of the submit object.

VALUE="buttonText" specifies the label to display on the button face.

To use a submit object's properties and methods:

1. `submitName.propertyName`
2. `submitName.methodName(parameters)`
3. `formName.elements[index].propertyName`
4. `formName.elements[index].methodName(parameters)`

`submitName`	the value of the NAME attribute of a submit object.
`formName`	either the value of the NAME attribute of a form object or an element in the forms array.
`index`	an integer representing a submit object on a form.
`propertyName`	one of the properties listed.
`methodName`	one of the methods listed.

Property Of   form

Description   A submit object is a form element and must be defined within a FORM tag. Clicking a submit button submits a form to the URL specified by the form's action property.

Properties   name reflects the NAME attribute
value reflects the VALUE attribute

Methods   click

Event Handlers   onClick

Example   The following example creates a submit object called submit_button with "Done" on its face.

```
<INPUT TYPE="submit" NAME="submit_button" VALUE="Done">
```

See Also   button, form, reset objects; submit method; onSubmit event handler

tan

Method

This Math method, Math.tan(*number*), calculates the tangent of its argument (an angle in radians).

target

Property

When used with a form, such as, myForm.target, the target contains the name of the window to receive responses after a form has been submitted. When used with a link, such as, link[0].target, the target contains the name of the window to receive contents of a clicked hypertext link.

text

Object

The text object is an HTML INPUT input field of type "text" on a form. The following is an example that is initially blank and 25 characters wide:

```
<B>ISP:</B> <INPUT TYPE="text" NAME="serviceProvider"
  VALUE="" SIZE=25>
```

Syntax A text object is defined using the HTML INPUT tag along with optional onBlur, on Change, onFocus, and onSelect event handlers:

```
<INPUT
  TYPE="text"
  NAME="textName"
  VALUE="textValue"
  SIZE=integer
  [onBlur="handlerText"]
  [onChange="handlerText"]
  [onFocus="handlerText"]
  [onSelect="handlerText"]>
```

NAME	the name of the text object	
VALUE	the initial value of the text object	
SIZE	the number of characters the text object can display without scrolling	

Property Of form

Properties

defaultValue	the initial VALUE attribute
name	the NAME attribute
value	the current VALUE attribute

Methods

```
focus
blur
select
```

Event Handlers

```
onBlur
onChange
onFocus
onSelect
```

See Also form, password, string, textarea objects

text

Property

A text property of the options array is the name of an option and consists of the string of text following an OPTION tag in a select object. In the following example, Red, Green, Blue, and Black are text properties of four options in a select object named mySelect. Initially one option, Red, will be shown; the others will appear when the object is clicked:

```
<FORM name="myForm">
  <SELECT NAME="mySelect">
    <OPTION SELECTED> Red
    <OPTION> Green
```

```
      <OPTION> Blue
      <OPTION> Black
   </SELECT>
   </FORM>
```

Options may be accessed for printing, for example, by using indexing over the options array as shown in the following code:

```
document.write("<P>" + "Number of options: " +
   document.myForm.mySelect.length)
for (var I = 0; I < document.myForm.mySelect.length; I++) {
   document.write("<P>" + "text[" + I + "]: " +
   document.myForm.mySelect.options[I].text)
   }
```

textarea

Object

A textarea object is a property of a form and is a scroll box for larger amounts of data or text than are practical to present all at once. Setting the size of the scroll box is part of the definition.

Syntax   A textarea object is defined in the standard HTML TEXTAREA tag along with optional onBlur, onChange, onFocus, and onSelect event handlers:

```
<TEXTAREA
   NAME="myTextareae"
   ROWS="nrows"
   COLS="ncols"
   WRAP="off|virtual|physical"
   [onBlur="myHandler"]
   [onChange="myHandler"]
   [onFocus="myHandler"]
   [onSelect="myHandler"]>
   whatToSee
</TEXTAREA>
```

NAME	the name of the textarea object
ROWS, COLS	the number of rows and columns in the scroll box
whatToSee	the initial textarea contents (ASCII text with optional newlines)
WRAP	"off" for lines displayed exactly as typed "virtual" wraps in the display
	"physical" wraps in the display and sends newlines at wrap points

The textarea can be accessed directly or as a form element, as illustrated in the following examples:

```
document.write("<P>" + "myTextarea name: " +
   document.myForm.myTextarea.name)
   document.write("<P>" + "myForm.elements[0]: " +
   document.myForm.elements[0].name)
```

Property Of   form

Properties   defaultValue   the VALUE attribute
name   the NAME attribute
value   the current value of the textarea object

Methods   blur
focus
select

Event Handlers   onBlur
onChange
onFocus
onSelect

See Also   form, password, string, text objects

title

Property

This document property, document.title, is a string containing the title of a document as assigned by HTML TITLE tags.

toGMTString

Method

For the user-defined Date object myDate, the method myDate.toGMTString() converts myDate to a string according to Internet GMT conventions, in other words, to GMT.

See Also Date object, toLocaleString method

toLocaleString

Method

For the user-defined Date object myDate, the method myDate.toLocaleString() converts myDate to a string according to the current locale conventions, that is, local time.

See Also Date object, toGMTString method

unescape

Function

This built-in function provides code conversion from numeric or "escaped" characters to their keyboard equivalent. For example, the following statement returns an ampersand (&).

```
unescape("%26")
```

userAgent

Property

This navigator property, navigator.userAgent, contains the value of the user-agent header sent in the HTTP protocol from client to server.

UTC

Method

This is a Date method, Date.UTC(*year*, *month*, *day* [, *hrs*] [, *min*] [, *sec*]), to convert comma-delimited date parameters into the number of milliseconds since January 1, 1970, 00:00:00, Universal Coordinated Time (GMT).

See Also Date object, parse method

value

Property

For objects of forms, such as, button, text, textarea, and so forth, the value property contains the VALUE attribute of the object.

Values

JavaScript recognizes the following variable and literal types:

- Numbers, such as 42 or 3.14159
- Logical (Boolean) values, either true or false
- Strings, such as "Howdy!"
- null, a special keyword denoting an empty string

This relatively small set of types of values, or data types, enables construction of many useful functions. Notice that there is no explicit distinction between integer- and real-valued or floating-point numbers. Nor is there an explicit date data type in Navigator. However, the Date object and its related built-in functions enable handling of dates.

Objects and functions are the other fundamental elements in the language. You can think of objects as named containers for values, and functions as procedures that your application can perform.

var

This is a programming keyword for declaring the type and the scope of variables. A variable that is to have the same meaning throughout an HTML document is considered global. It should be declared by a var statement in the HTML HEAD before the definition of any functions.

JavaScript is a loosely typed language. That means that you do not have to declare the data type of a variable before you use it, and data types are converted automatically as needed during the course of script execution. So, for example, you could declare a variable as apparently integer:

```
var answer = 42
```

and later use the same variable to store a string, such as

```
answer = "Thanks for all the fish..."
```

In addition, in expressions involving numeric and string values, JavaScript converts the numeric values to strings. Thus, in the statements:

```
x = "The answer is " + 42
y = 42 + " is the answer"
```

x will be "The answer is 42" and y will be "42 is the answer." There are special functions going the other way, that is, for converting strings to values. See "eval" for attempting general conversion, "parseInt" for converting a string to an integer of a specified radix (base), and "parseFloat" for converting a string to a floating-point number.

Variables

The identifier or name of a JavaScript variable must start with a letter or underscore ("_") and may continue with digits (0–9) or letters (the characters "A" through "Z" [uppercase] and the characters "a" through "z" [lowercase]). JavaScript is case-sensitive. Examples include Number_hits, temp99, and _name.

Variable Scope

The scope of a variable is where you can use it in a script. In JavaScript, there are two scopes that a variable can have:

- Global: you can use the variable anywhere in the application.
- Local: you can use the variable within the current function.

To declare a local variable inside a function, use the var keyword, for example,

```
var total = 0
```

To declare a global variable, declare the variable by assignment; that is, simply assign the desired value to the variable (either in a function or outside a function), for example,

```
total = 0
```

It is good programming practice to declare global variables at the beginning of your script so that functions will inherit the variable and its value.

vlinkColor

Property

This document property, document.vlinkColor, is a string specifying the color of visited links. The string consists of a hexadecimal RGB triplet or a color name literal and is the VLINK attribute of the HTML BODY tag.

while

Programming Keyword

This is a programming keyword for creating a loop.

Syntax
```
while (conditional expression) {
    loop code
    }
```

See Also   do while, for (programming keywords)

with

This is a programming keyword for abbreviating an object reference. Use it with Math, for example, when a section of code uses several math constants and methods so that you don't have to type "Math" repeatedly.

Example
```
with (Math) {
    a = PI * r*r;
    y = r*sin(theta)
    x = r*cos(theta)
    }
```

window

A JavaScript program inherits a window that has been prepared by the browser or navigator according to an HTML document. Parameters or properties associated with this top window and the object's document, history, location, and navigator provide access to the environment in which the program begins running.

Syntax
To define a new window use the open method:
```
myWindow = window.open("URL", "windowName"
    [,"windowFeatures"])
```

`myWindow`	the name of the new window.
`WindowName`	the window name to use as the TARGET of a FORM or A tag.

To use a window object's properties and methods:

1. `window.propertyName`
2. `window.methodName(parameters)`
3. `self.propertyName`
4. `self.methodName(parameters)`
5. `top.propertyName`
6. `top.methodName(parameters)`

7. `parent.propertyName`

8. `parent.methodName(parameters)`

9. `myWindow.propertyName`

10. `myWindow.methodName(parameters)`

11. `propertyName`

12. `methodName(parameters)`

Optional onLoad or onUnload event handlers for a window object may be defined in the BODY or FRAMESET tags:

```
<BODY
   . . .
   [onLoad="myHandler"]
   [onUnload="myHandler"]>
</BODY>
<FRAMESET
   ROWS="rowHeightList"
   COLS="columnWidthList"
   [onLoad="myHandler"]
   [onUnload="myHandler"]>
   [<FRAME SRC="myURL" NAME="myFrame">]
</FRAMESET>
```

Description   The window object is the top-level object in the JavaScript client hierarchy.

A JavaScript program may refer to the current window by name or by the synonyms self and window. For example, you can close the current window by either window.close() or self.close().
The top and parent are also synonyms that refer, respectively, to the initial Navigator window and to the one that called the current window.

Properties

defaultStatus	the default message displayed in the Navigator's status bar
frames	the array containing all the frames in a window
length	the number of frames in a parent window
name	the target name of the window
parent	a synonym for a window name; refers to a window containing a frameset

self	a synonym for the current window
status	a priority or transient message in the Navigator's status bar
top	a synonym for the topmost Navigator window
window	a synonym for the current window

The following objects are also properties of the window object:

document
frame
location

Methods

```
alert
close
confirm
open
prompt
setTimeout
```

Event Handlers

```
onLoad
onUnload
```

Examples The Navigator displays a document in its initial or top window. The following document opens and loads a second window immediately, and by way of a form with buttons it enables the viewer to open and close a third window that is blank except for output.

```
<BODY BGCOLOR="aquamarine">
<SCRIPT>
myWindow2=open("window2_ex.htm","secondWindow","scrollbars=yes")
document.writeln("<BR><B>Top window location: " +
  window.location + "</B>")
document.writeln("<BR><B>Second window location: " +
  myWindow2.location + "</B>")
document.writeln("<BR><B>Second window name : " +
  myWindow2.name + "</B>")
</SCRIPT>
<FORM NAME="myForm">
<P><INPUT TYPE="button" VALUE="Open output window"
onClick="myWindow3=window.open('','outputWindow','scrollbars=yes')">
```

```
<P><INPUT TYPE="button" VALUE="Send some output"
  onClick="myWindow3.document.writeln('Testing
  ...');myWindow3.document.close()">
<P><INPUT TYPE="button" VALUE="Close output window"
  onClick="myWindow3.close()">
<P><INPUT TYPE="button" VALUE="Close second window"
  onClick="myWindow2.close()">
</FORM>
```

Code for the second window illustrates the self synonym:

```
<BODY BGCOLOR="lightblue"
  onLoad  ="alert('Window name: ' + window.name + ' Testing
  ...')"
  onUnload="alert('Window name: ' + window.name + ' Closing
  ...')">
<SCRIPT LANGUAGE="JAVASCRIPT">
document.writeln("<BR><B>Second window location: " +
  self.location + "</B>")
document.writeln("<BR><B>Second window name : " + self.name +
  "</B>")
</SCRIPT>
```

See Also   document, frame objects

window

The window property is a synonym for the current window or frame.

write, writeln

Either of these methods writes one or more expressions to a document in the specified window. The writeln method is the same as the write method, except that the writeln method appends a newline character to the end of the output. The output is sent to the client computer's display only; JavaScript does not permit writing to the client's file system.

Syntax document.write(*expression1* [,*expression2*], ...[,*expressionN*])

expression1 through *expressionN* are any JavaScript expressions or the properties of existing objects.

Method Of document

Description The write method displays any number of expressions in a document window. An expression may including numerics, strings, or logicals. Numeric expressions will be converted to strings before printing. Logical expressions will be converted to true or false. The entire argument list will be automatically concatenated into a single string before printing. The plus operator (+) may also be used along with descriptive labels or literals for easier-to-read results. For example,

```
document.write("<P>" + " (25 < 50) = " + (25 < 50))
document.write("<P>" + " (25 / 50) = " + (25 / 50))
document.write("<P>" + " Math.sqrt(64) = " + Math.sqrt(64))
document.write("<P>", " sin(PI), cos(PI) = ",
    Math.sin(Math.PI), ", ", Math.cos(Math.PI))
```

Output with write or writeln may be placed within any SCRIPT tag or within an event handler.

See Also close, clear, open methods

III Appendices

This part provides a quick reference to JavaScript objects, arrays, properties, methods, event handlers, and programming keywords. For additional reference, see the Netscape JavaScript Authoring Guide at http://home.netscape.com/eng/mozilla/3.0/handbook/javascript/index.html.

Appendix A
About the Companion CD-ROM

The CD-ROM included with your copy of *The HTML Programmer's Reference* contains the entire text of the book in hypertext format.

To view the CD-ROM:

- **Windows:** Double-click on LAUNCHME.EXE.
- **Macintosh:** Double-click on LAUNCHME.

You'll see a menu screen offering several choices. See "Navigating the CD-ROM" below for your option choices.

If the viewer does not run properly on your machine, follow these instructions for optimum performance:

WINDOWS

1. Copy the LAUNCHME.EXE and LAUNCHME.INI files to the same directory on your hard drive.
2. Open the LAUNCHME.INI file in a text editor such as Notepad.
3. Find the section in the .INI file that reads:

   ```
   [Memory]
   ;ExtraMemory=400
   ; Amount of kBytes over and above physical memory for
   use by a projector.
   ```

4. If your computer has enough memory to do so, delete the semicolon from the ExtraMemory line, and change the ExtraMemory setting to a higher number.
5. Save the changes to the LAUNCHME.INI file, and close the text editor.

6. With the CD-ROM still inserted, launch the viewer from the hard drive.

If the viewer still does not run properly on your machine, you can access the material on the CD-ROM directly through File Manager (Windows 3.x) or Windows Explorer (Windows 95).

MACINTOSH

1. Copy the Launch Me file to your hard drive.

2. Click once on the Launch Me file.

3. Select Get Info from the File menu.

4. If your computer has enough memory to do so, change the amount in the Preferred size field to a higher number.

5. Close the info box.

6. With the CD-ROM still inserted, launch the viewer from the hard drive.

If the viewer still does not run properly, you can access the material on the CD directly by double-clicking on the CD's icon on your desktop.

NAVIGATING THE CD-ROM

Your choices for navigating the CD-ROM appear on the opening screen. You can investigate the book's contents in From the Book, browse the Hot Picks, learn more about Ventana, or quit the CD.

When you click on From the Book, you will be presented with two choices: Locate Browser and Launch Browser. You must click on Locate Browser first, and help the program find your Web browser. You will not have to perform this step again unless you move your Web browser to another directory or another hard drive. You can then click on Launch Browser and your browser will launch and open up a fully hyperlinked version of the book.

TECHNICAL SUPPORT

Technical support is available for installation-related problems only. The technical support office is open from 8:00 A.M. to 6:00 P.M. Monday through Friday and can be reached via the following methods:

- Phone: (919) 544-9404 extension 81
- Faxback Answer System: (919) 544-9404 extension 85
- E-mail: help@vmedia.com
- FAX: (919) 544-9472
- World Wide Web: **http://www.vmedia.com/support**
- America Online: keyword *Ventana*

LIMITS OF LIABILITY & DISCLAIMER OF WARRANTY

The authors and publisher of this book have used their best efforts in preparing the CD-ROM and the programs contained in it. These efforts include the development, research, and testing of the theories and programs to determine their effectiveness. The authors and publisher make no warranty of any kind expressed or implied, with regard to these programs or the documentation contained in this book.

The authors and publisher shall not be liable in the event of incidental or consequential damages in connection with, or arising out of, the furnishing, performance, or use of the programs, associated instructions, and/or claims of productivity gains.

Appendix B
Color Code Tables

These color tables show you all of the colors that can be displayed by most modern browsers. The table lists all colors in two different sorts: by Hex Value and by Color Name.

The two columns on the left of the table show you the Hex value. Use these two columns when you want to specify a *known* color, in Hex format.

The two columns on the right of the tables are sorted so that you can find any color's name based on the *known* Hex value.

My thanks to the anonymous originators of some of these color names. Alas, most of these unusual color names are simply for your reference purposes only and cannot be expected to be rendered by most browsers.

TRAP

Proper color names vary with the browser. Hex values do not! Also, be aware that colors are rendered differently on varying computer monitors. Don't expect users to differentiate between two shades that are only subtly different in color.

Hex Color Values Sorted by Color Name		Color Names Sorted by Hex Value	
Look up the Color Name here:	*Find the Hex Value here:*	*Look up the Hex Value here:*	*Find the Color Name Here:*
White	#FFFFFF	#000000	Black
Red	#FF0000	#00009C	New Midnight Blue
Green	#00FF00	#0000FF	Blue
Blue	#0000FF	#007FFF	Slate Blue
Magenta	#FF00FF	#00FF00	Green
Cyan	#00FFFF	#00FF7F	Spring Green
Yellow	#FFFF00	#00FFFF	Cyan
Black	#000000	#215E21	Hunter Green
Aquamarine	#70DB93	#23238E	Navy Blue
Baker's Chocolate	#5C3317	#236B8E	Steel Blue
Blue Violet	#9F5F9F	#238E23	Forest Green
Brass	#B5A642	#238E68	Sea Green
Bright Gold	#D9D919	#2F2F4F	Midnight Blue
Brown	#A62A2A	#2F4F2F	Dark Green
Bronze	#8C7853	#2F4F4F	Dark Slate Gray
Bronze II	#A67D3D	#3232CD	Medium Blue
Cadet Blue	#5F9F9F	#3299CC	Sky Blue
Cool Copper	#D98719	#32CD32	Lime Green
Copper	#B87333	#32CD99	Medium Aquamarine
Coral	#FF7F00	#38B0DE	Summer Sky
Corn Flower Blue	#42426F	#42426F	Corn Flower Blue
Dark Brown	#5C4033	#426F42	Medium Sea Green
Dark Green	#2F4F2F	#4A766E	Dark Green Copper
Dark Green Copper	#4A766E	#4D4DFF	Neon Blue
Dark Olive Green	#4F4F2F	#4E2F2F	Indian Red
Dark Orchid	#9932CD	#4F2F4F	Violet
Dark Purple	#871F78	#4F4F2F	Dark Olive Green

➡

Hex Color Values Sorted by Color Name		Color Names Sorted by Hex Value	
Look up the Color Name here:	*Find the Hex Value here:*	*Look up the Hex Value here:*	*Find the Color Name Here:*
Dark Slate Blue	#6B238E	#527F76	Green Copper
Dark Slate Gray	#2F4F4F	#545454	Dim Gray
Dark Tan	#97694F	#5959AB	Rich Blue
Dark Turquoise	#7093DB	#5C3317	Baker's Chocolate
Dark Wood	#855E42	#5C4033	Dark Brown
Dim Gray	#545454	#5C4033	Very Dark Brown
Dusty Rose	#856363	#5F9F9F	Cadet Blue
Feldspar	#D19275	#6B238E	Dark Slate Blue
Firebrick	#8E2323	#6B4226	Semi-Sweet Chocolate
Forest Green	#238E23	#6B8E23	Medium Forest Green
Gold	#CD7F32	#6F4242	Salmon
Goldenrod	#DBDB70	#7093DB	Dark Turquoise
Gray	#C0C0C0	#70DB93	Aquamarine
Green Copper	#527F76	#70DBDB	Medium Turquoise
Green Yellow	#93DB70	#7F00FF	Medium Slate Blue
Hunter Green	#215E21	#7FFF00	Medium Spring Green
Indian Red	#4E2F2F	#855E42	Dark Wood
Khaki	#9F9F5F	#856363	Dusty Rose
Light Blue	#C0D9D9	#871F78	Dark Purple
Light Gray	#A8A8A8	#8C1717	Scarlet
Light Steel Blue	#8F8FBD	#8C7853	Bronze
Light Wood	#E9C2A6	#8E2323	Firebrick
Lime Green	#32CD32	#8E236B	Maroon
Mandarin Orange	#E47833	#8E6B23	Sienna
Maroon	#8E236B	#8F8FBD	Light Steel Blue
Medium Aquamarine	#32CD99	#8FBC8F	Pale Green
Medium Blue	#3232CD	#9370DB	Medium Orchid

➡

Hex Color Values Sorted by Color Name		Color Names Sorted by Hex Value	
Look up the Color Name here:	*Find the Hex Value here:*	*Look up the Hex Value here:*	*Find the Color Name Here:*
Medium Forest Green	#6B8E23	#93DB70	Green Yellow
Medium Goldenrod	#EAEAAE	#97694F	Dark Tan
Medium Orchid	#9370DB	#9932CD	Dark Orchid
Medium Sea Green	#426F42	#99CC32	Yellow Green
Medium Slate Blue	#7F00FF	#9F5F9F	Blue Violet
Medium Spring Green	#7FFF00	#9F9F5F	Khaki
Medium Turquoise	#70DBDB	#A62A2A	Brown
Medium Violet Red	#DB7093	#A67D3D	Bronze II
Medium Wood	#A68064	#A68064	Medium Wood
Midnight Blue	#2F2F4F	#A8A8A8	Light Gray
Navy Blue	#23238E	#ADEAEA	Turquoise
Neon Blue	#4D4DFF	#B5A642	Brass
Neon Pink	#FF6EC7	#B87333	Copper
New Midnight Blue	#00009C	#BC8F8F	Pink
New Tan	#EBC79E	#C0C0C0	Gray
Old Gold	#CFB53B	#C0D9D9	Light Blue
Orange	#FF7F00	#CC3299	Violet Red
Orange Red	#FF2400	#CD7F32	Gold
Orchid	#DB70DB	#CDCDCD	Very Light Gray
Pale Green	#8FBC8F	#CFB53B	Old Gold
Pink	#BC8F8F	#D19275	Feldspar
Plum	#EAADEA	#D8BFD8	Thistle
Quartz	#D9D9F3	#D8D8BF	Wheat
Rich Blue	#5959AB	#D98719	Cool Copper
Salmon	#6F4242	#D9D919	Bright Gold
Scarlet	#8C1717	#D9D9F3	Quartz
Sea Green	#238E68	#DB7093	Medium Violet Red

➡

Hex Color Values Sorted by Color Name		Color Names Sorted by Hex Value	
Look up the Color Name here:	*Find the Hex Value here:*	*Look up the Hex Value here:*	*Find the Color Name Here:*
Semi-Sweet Chocolate	#6B4226	#DB70DB	Orchid
Sienna	#8E6B23	#DB9370	Tan
Silver	#E6E8FA	#DBDB70	Goldenrod
Sky Blue	#3299CC	#E47833	Mandarin Orange
Slate Blue	#007FFF	#E6E8FA	Silver
Spicy Pink	#FF1CAE	#E9C2A6	Light Wood
Spring Green	#00FF7F	#EAADEA	Plum
Steel Blue	#236B8E	#EAEAAE	Medium Goldenrod
Summer Sky	#38B0DE	#EBC79E	New Tan
Tan	#DB9370	#FF0000	Red
Thistle	#D8BFD8	#FF00FF	Magenta
Turquoise	#ADEAEA	#FF1CAE	Spicy Pink
Very Dark Brown	#5C4033	#FF2400	Orange Red
Very Light Gray	#CDCDCD	#FF6EC7	Neon Pink
Violet	#4F2F4F	#FF7F00	Coral
Violet Red	#CC3299	#FF7F00	Orange
Wheat	#D8D8BF	#FFFF00	Yellow
Yellow Green	#99CC32	#FFFFFF	White

Appendix C
ISO Tables

ISO LATIN-1 CHARACTER SET

HTML authors will often find reference to the ISO Latin-1 Character Set for both research and easier reading. Netscape Navigator is pre-configured by default to use this character set, so it's a *good* reference to keep at hand—especially if you're creating multiple language versions of your documents.

This table is sorted by *Character*.

Character	HTML Code	Produces
Á	Á	Capital A, with acute accent
á	á	Small a, with acute accent
À	À	Capital A, with grave accent
à	à	Small a, with grave accent
Â	Â	Capital A, with circumflex
â	â	Small a, with circumflex
Ä	Ä	Capital A, with dieresis / umlaut
ä	ä	Small a, with dieresis / umlaut
Ã	Ã	Capital A, with tilde
ã	ã	Small a, with tilde
Å	Å	Capital A, with ring
å	å	Small a, with ring
Æ	Æ	Capital AE ligature
æ	æ	Small ae ligature
Ç	Ç	Capital C, with cedilla

Character	HTML Code	Produces
ç	&#231;	Small c, with cedilla
Ð	&#208;	Capital Eth, Icelandic
ð	&#240;	Small eth, Icelandic
É	&#201;	Capital E, with acute accent
é	&#233;	Small e, with acute accent
È	&#200;	Capital E, with grave accent
è	&#232;	Small e, with grave accent
Ê	&#202;	Capital E, with circumflex
ê	&#234;	Small e, with circumflex
Ë	&#203;	Capital E, with dieresis / umlaut
ë	&#235;	Small e, with dieresis / umlaut
Í	&#205;	Capital I, with acute accent
í	&#237;	Small i, with acute accent
Ì	&#204;	Capital I, with grave accent
ì	&#236;	Small i, with grave accent
Î	&#206;	Capital I, with circumflex
î	&#238;	Small i, with circumflex
Ï	&#207;	Capital I, with dieresis / umlaut
ï	&#239;	Small i, with dieresis / umlaut
Ñ	&#209;	Capital N, with tilde
ñ	&#241;	Small n, with tilde
Ó	&#211;	Capital O, with acute accent
ó	&#243;	Small o, with acute accent
Ò	&#210;	Capital O, with grave accent
ò	&#242;	Small o, with grave accent
Ô	&#212;	Capital O, with circumflex
ô	&#244;	Small o, with circumflex
Ö	&#214;	Capital O, with dieresis / umlaut
ö	&#246;	Small o, with dieresis / umlaut
Õ	&#213;	Capital O, with tilde

Character	HTML Code	Produces
õ	&#245;	Small o, with tilde
Ø	&#216;	Capital O, with slash
ø	&#248;	Small o, with slash
ß	&#223;	Small sharp s, with German sz
Þ	&#222;	Capital Thorn, Icelandic
þ	&#254;	Small thorn, Icelandic
Ú	&#218;	Capital U, with acute accent
ú	&#250;	Small u, with acute accent
Ù	&#217;	Capital U, with grave accent
ù	&#249;	Small u, with grave accent
Û	&#219;	Capital U, with circumflex
û	&#251;	Small u, with circumflex
Ü	&#220;	Capital U, with dieresis / umlaut
ü	&#252;	Small u, with dieresis / umlaut
Y	&#221;	Capital Y, with acute accent
ý	&#253;	Small y, with acute accent
ÿ	&#255;	Small y, with dieresis / umlaut

COMPLETE ISO CHARACTER SET

This table is the whole enchilada! The complete ISO Character Set. Refer to this table whenever you need to display a non-standard character, or when you simply need to display characters that don't normally occur in the English (US) language.

Unlike the Latin ISO table in this book, the Complete ISO Character Set is sorted by the description of the character in the "Produces" column. When you know the "name" of the character, try running down the "Produces" list to locate the ISO character.

This table is sorted by the description found in the "Produces" column.

Character	HTML Code	Produces
'	&#96;	Acute accent
´	&#180;	Acute accent
&	&#38;	Ampersand
'	&#39;	Apostrophe
*	&#42;	Asterisk
¦	&#166;	Broken vertical bar
A	&#65;	Capital A
Á	&#193;	Capital A, with acute accent
Â	&#194;	Capital A, with circumflex
Ä	&#196;	Capital A, with dieresis / umlaut
À	&#192;	Capital A, with grave accent
Å	&#197;	Capital A, with ring
Ã	&#195;	Capital A, with tilde
Æ	&#198;	Capital AE ligature
B	&#66;	Capital B
C	&#67;	Capital C
Ç	&#199;	Capital C, with cedilla
D	&#68;	Capital D

➡

Character	HTML Code	Produces
E	&#69;	Capital E
É	&#201;	Capital E, with acute accent
Ê	&#202;	Capital E, with circumflex
Ë	&#203;	Capital E, with dieresis / umlaut
È	&#200;	Capital E, with grave accent
Ð	&#208;	Capital Eth, Icelandic
F	&#70;	Capital F
G	&#71;	Capital G
H	&#72;	Capital H
I	&#73;	Capital I
Í	&#205;	Capital I, with acute accent
Î	&#206;	Capital I, with circumflex
Ï	&#207;	Capital I, with dieresis / umlaut
Ì	&#204;	Capital I, with grave accent
J	&#74;	Capital J
K	&#75;	Capital K
L	&#76;	Capital L
M	&#77;	Capital M
N	&#78;	Capital N
Ñ	&#209;	Capital N, with tilde
O	&#79;	Capital O
Ó	&#211;	Capital O, with acute accent
Ô	&#212;	Capital O, with circumflex
Ö	&#214;	Capital O, with dieresis / umlaut
Ò	&#210;	Capital O, with grave accent
Ø	&#216;	Capital O, with slash
Õ	&#213;	Capital O, with tilde
Œ	&#140;	Capital OE ligature
P	&#80;	Capital P
Q	&#81;	Capital Q

Character	HTML Code	Produces
R	R	Capital R
S	S	Capital S
Š	Š	Capital S, with hacek
T	T	Capital T
Þ	Þ	Capital Thorn, Icelandic
U	U	Capital U
Ú	Ú	Capital U, with acute accent
Û	Û	Capital U, with circumflex
Ü	Ü	Capital U, with dieresis / umlaut
Ù	Ù	Capital U, with grave accent
V	V	Capital V
W	W	Capital W
X	X	Capital X
Y	Y	Capital Y
Y	Ý	Capital Y, with acute accent
Ÿ	Ÿ	Capital Y, with dieresis / umlaut
Z	Z	Capital Z
^	^	Caret
ˆ	ˆ	Caret
		Carriage Return
¸	¸	Cedilla
¢	¢	Cent sign
:	:	Colon
,	,	Comma
@	@	Commercial at
©	©	Copyright
†	†	Dagger
°	°	Degree sign
¨	¨	Dieresis / Umlaut
0	0	Digit 0

Character	HTML Code	Produces
1	&#49;	Digit 1
2	&#50;	Digit 2
3	&#51;	Digit 3
4	&#52;	Digit 4
5	&#53;	Digit 5
6	&#54;	Digit 6
7	&#55;	Digit 7
8	&#56;	Digit 8
9	&#57;	Digit 9
÷	&#247;	Division sign
$	&#36;	Dollar sign
·	&#149;	Dot, middle
"	&#147;	Double beginning quotation mark
‡	&#135;	Double dagger
"	&#148;	Double ending quotation mark
…	&#133;	Ellipses
—	&#151;	Em dash
–	&#150;	En dash
=	&#61;	Equals sign
!	&#33;	Exclamation mark
ª	&#170;	Feminine ordinal
¼	&#188;	Fraction, one-fourth
½	&#189;	Fraction, one-half
¾	&#190;	Fraction, three-fourths
f	&#131;	Function sign
¤	&#164;	General currency sign
>	&#62;	Greater than
›	&#155;	Greater-than sign
—	&#95;	Horizontal bar
	&#09;	Horizontal tab

Character	HTML Code	Produces
-	&#45;	Hyphen
¡	&#161;	Inverted exclamation
¿	&#191;	Inverted question mark
«	&#171;	Left angle quote, with guillemot left
{	&#123;	Left curly brace
(	&#40;	Left parenthesis
[	&#91;	Left square bracket
<	&#60;	Less than
‹	&#139;	Less-than sign
	&#10;	Line feed
„	&#132;	Low double-comma quotation mark
‚	&#130;	Low single-comma quotation mark
¯	&#175;	Macron accent
º	&#186;	Masculine ordinal
µ	&#181;	Micro sign
·	&#183;	Middle dot
x	&#215;	Multiply sign
		Non-breaking Space
¬	&#172;	Not sign
#	&#35;	Number sign
¶	&#182;	Paragraph sign
‰	&#137;	Per mile sign
%	&#37;	Percent sign
.	&#46;	Period (fullstop)
±	&#177;	Plus or minus
+	&#43;	Plus sign
£	&#163;	Pound sterling
?	&#63;	Question mark
"	&#34;	Quotation mark
®	&#174;	Registered trademark

Character	HTML Code	Produces
\	&#92;	Reverse solidus (backslash)
»	&#187;	Right angle quote, with guillemot right
}	&#125;	Right curly brace
)	&#41;	Right parenthesis
]	&#93;	Right square bracket
§	&#167;	Section sign
;	&#59;	Semi-colon
'	&#145;	Single beginning quotation mark
'	&#146;	Single ending quotation mark
a	&#97;	Small a
á	&#225;	Small a, with acute accent
â	&#226;	Small a, with circumflex
ä	&#228;	Small a, with dieresis / umlaut
à	&#224;	Small a, with grave accent
å	&#229;	Small a, with ring
ã	&#227;	Small a, with tilde
æ	&#230;	Small ae ligature
b	&#98;	Small b
c	&#99;	Small c
ç	&#231;	Small c, cedilla
d	&#100;	Small d
e	&#101;	Small e
é	&#233;	Small e, with acute accent
ê	&#234;	Small e, with circumflex
ë	&#235;	Small e, with dieresis / umlaut
è	&#232;	Small e, with grave accent
ð	&#240;	Small eth, Icelandic
f	&#102;	Small f
g	&#103;	Small g
h	&#104;	Small h

Character	HTML Code	Produces
i	&#105;	Small I
í	&#237;	Small i, with acute accent
î	&#238;	Small i, with circumflex
ï	&#239;	Small i, with dieresis / umlaut
ì	&#236;	Small i, with grave accent
j	&#106;	Small j
k	&#107;	Small k
l	&#108;	Small l
m	&#109;	Small m
n	&#110;	Small n
ñ	&#241;	Small n, with tilde
o	&#111;	Small o
ó	&#243;	Small o, with acute accent
ô	&#244;	Small o, with circumflex
ö	&#246;	Small o, with dieresis / umlaut
ò	&#242;	Small o, with grave accent
ø	&#248;	Small o, with slash
õ	&#245;	Small o, with tilde
œ	&#156;	Small oe ligature
p	&#112;	Small p
q	&#113;	Small q
r	&#114;	Small r
s	&#115;	Small s
š	&#154;	Small s, with hacek
ß	&#223;	Small sharp s, with German sz
t	&#116;	Small t
þ	&#254;	Small thorn, Icelandic
u	&#117;	Small u
ú	&#250;	Small u, with acute accent
û	&#251;	Small u, with circumflex

Character	HTML Code	Produces
ü	&#252;	Small u, with dieresis / umlaut
ù	&#249;	Small u, with grave accent
v	&#118;	Small v
w	&#119;	Small w
x	&#120;	Small x
y	&#121;	Small y
ý	&#253;	Small y, with acute accent
ÿ	&#255;	Small y, with dieresis / umlaut
z	&#122;	Small z
–	&#173;	Soft hyphen
/	&#47;	Solidus (slash)
1	&#185;	Superscript one
3	&#179;	Superscript three
2	&#178;	Superscript two
~	&#126;	Tilde
˜	&#152;	Tilde
TM	&#153;	Trademark symbol
|	|	Vertical bar
¥	&#165;	Yen sign

Appendix D
Jump Tables

Okay, so you don't want to have to open the book, then thumb through to the point that holds your content—even if the content is sorted in an encyclopedic fashion. For those of you who prefer to use an index to find the content you seek, this appendix provides four simple jump tables that help you quickly jump to the page that holds content of interest to you.

And of course, not all brains work the same way! That's why this appendix provides two different ways to visually scroll through the jump tables. The first two tables reference Part I: HTML. The first table is an alphabetical sort by Tag and the second table sorts the same information by Type. The last two tables reference Part II: JavaScript. The first table is an alphabetical sort by Tag and the second table sorts the same information by Type.

PART I: HTML SORTED BY TAG

Tag	Type	Page
!	Structural Definition	1
A	Graphics/Links	2
ADDRESS	Structural Definition	4
APPLET	Graphics/Links	5
B	Presentation Formatting	9
BASE HREF	Graphics/Links	10
BASEFONT SIZE	Structural Definition	11
		➡

Tag	Type	Page
BGSOUND SRC	Miscellaneous	12
BIG	Structural Definition	13
BLINK	Presentation Formatting	14
BLOCKQUOTE	Structural Definition	15
BODY	Structural Definition	16
BR	Presentation Formatting	20
CAPTION	Tables	21
CENTER	Structural Definition	23
CITE	Structural Definition	24
CODE	Structural Definition	25
DD	Structural Definition	26
DFN	Structural Definition	27
DIR	Structural Definition	28
DIR TYPE	Lists	29
DIV	Structural Definition	30
DL	Lists	32
DT	Lists	34
EM	Structural Definition	35
EMBED	Graphics/Links	36
FONT	Presentation Formatting	38
FORM	Forms	41
FRAME	Frames	43
FRAMESET	Frames	47
H1	Structural Definition	49
H2	Structural Definition	50
H3	Structural Definition	51
H4	Structural Definition	52
H5	Structural Definition	53
H6	Structural Definition	54
HEAD	Structural Definition	55

➡

Tag	Type	Page
HR	Miscellaneous	56
HTML	Structural Definition	59
I	Presentation Formatting	60
IMG SRC	Graphics/Links	61
INPUT	Forms	67
ISINDEX	Forms	73
KBD	Structural Definition	75
LI	Structural Definition	76
LINK	Graphics/Links	78
LISTING	Structural Definition	80
MAP	Graphics/Links	81
MARQUEE	Miscellaneous	82
MENU	Structural Definition	87
META	Graphics/Links	88
MULTICOL	Miscellaneous	90
NOBR	Structural Definition	92
NOFRAMES	Miscellaneous	93
OL	Lists	94
OPTION	Forms	96
P	Structural Definition	98
PARAM	Miscellaneous	99
PLAINTEXT	Structural Definition	100
PRE	Structural Definition	101
S	Structural Definition	102
SAMP	Structural Definition	103
SCRIPT	Miscellaneous	104
SELECT	Forms	105
SMALL	Structural Definition	107
SPACER	Miscellaneous	108
STRIKE	Structural Definition	110

Tag	Type	Page
STRONG	Structural Definition	111
SUB	Structural Definition	112
SUP	Structural Definition	113
TABLE	Tables	114
TD	Tables	120
TEXTAREA	Forms	123
TH	Tables	125
TBODY	Structural Definition	128
TFOOT	Structural Definition	130
THEAD	Structural Definition	132
TITLE	Structural Definition	134
TR	Tables	135
TT	Presentation Formatting	136
U	Structural Definition	137
UL	Lists	138
VAR	Structural Definition	140
WBR	Structural Definition	141

PART I: HTML SORTED BY TYPE

Type	Tag	Page
Forms	FORM	41
	INPUT	67
	ISINDEX	73
	OPTION	96
	SELECT	105
	TEXTAREA	123
		➡

Type	Tag	Page
Frames	FRAME	43
	FRAMESET	47
Graphics/Links	A	2
	APPLET	5
	BASE HREF	10
	EMBED	36
	IMG SRC	61
	LINK	78
	MAP	81
	META	88
Lists	DIR TYPE	29
	DL	32
	DT	34
	OL	94
	UL	138
Miscellaneous	BGSOUND SRC	12
	HR	56
	MARQUEE	82
	MULTICOL	90
	NOFRAMES	93
	PARAM	99
	SCRIPT	104
	SPACER	108
Presentation Formatting	B	9
	BLINK	14
	BR	20
	FONT	38
	I	60
	TT	136

➡

Type	Tag	Page
Structural Definition	!	1
	ADDRESS	4
	BASEFONT SIZE	11
	BIG	13
	BLOCKQUOTE	15
	BODY	16
	CENTER	23
	CITE	24
	CODE	25
	DD	26
	DFN	27
	DIR	28
	DIV	30
	EM	35
	H1	49
	H2	50
	H3	51
	H4	52
	H5	53
	H6	54
	HEAD	55
	HTML	59
	KBD	75
	LI	76
	LISTING	80
	MENU	87
	NOBR	92
	P	98
	PLAINTEXT	100
	PRE	101

➡

Type	Tag	Page
	S	102
	SAMP	103
	SMALL	107
	STRIKE	110
	STRONG	111
	SUB	112
	SUP	113
	TBODY	128
	TFOOT	130
	THEAD	132
	TITLE	134
	U	137
	VAR	140
	WBR	141
Tables	CAPTION	21
	TABLE	114
	TD	120
	TH	125
	TR	135

PART II: JAVASCRIPT SORTED BY TAG

Tag	Type	Page
abs	Method	145
acos	Method	145
action	Property	145
alert	Method	145
alinkColor	Property	146

➡

Tag	Type	Page
anchor	Method	146
anchor	Object	146
appCodeName	Property	147
appName	Property	147
appVersion	Property	147
array	Object	147
asin	Method	148
atan	Method	148
back	Method	149
bgColor	Property	149
big	Method	149
blink	Method	150
blur	Method	150
bold	Method	150
break	Programming Keyword	151
button	Object	151
ceil	Method	152
charAt	Method	152
checkbox	Object	152
checked	Property	154
clear	Method	154
clearTimeout	Method	155
click	Method	155
close	Method	155
close	Method	156
confirm	Method	156
continue	Programming Keyword	156
cookie	Property	156
cos	Method	157
Date	Object	157

➡

Tag	Type	Page
defaultChecked	Property	158
defaultSelected	Property	159
defaultStatus	Property	159
defaultValue	Property	159
do while	Programming Keyword	162
document	Object	160
E	Property	162
elements array	Property	162
encoding	Property	163
escape	Function	163
eval	Function	163
exp	Method	164
fgColor	Property	164
floor	Method	165
focus	Method	165
fontcolor	Method	165
fontsize	Method	166
for	Programming Keyword	166
form	Object (forms array)	166
forward	Method	168
frame	Object (frames array)	169
function	Programming Keyword	170
getDate	Method	170
getDay	Method	171
getHours	Method	171
getMinutes	Method	171
getMonth	Method	171
getSeconds	Method	172
getTime	Method	172
getTimezoneOffset	Method	172

Tag	Type	Page
getYear	Method	172
go	Method	173
hash	Property	173
hidden	Object	173
history	Object	175
host	Property	177
hostname	Property	177
href	Property	177
if	Programming Keyword	177
if ... else	Programming Keyword	178
index	Property	178
indexOf	Method	178
isNaN	Function	179
italics	Method	179
lastIndexOf	Method	179
length	Property	180
link	Method	181
link	Object (links array)	182
linkColor	Property	181
LN10	Property	183
LN2	Property	183
location	Object	184
location	Property	185
log	Method	185
LOG10E	Property	185
LOG2E	Property	185
Math	Object	185
max	Method	187
method	Property	187
min	Method	187

➡

Tag	Type	Page
navigator	Object	187
new	Programming Keyword	188
onBlur	Event Handler	188
onChange	Event Handler	189
onClick	Event Handler	189
onFocus	Event Handler	190
onLoad	Event Handler	190
onMouseOver	Event Handler	191
onSelect	Event Handler	191
onSubmit	Event Handler	192
onUnload	Event Handler	192
open	Method (document object)	193
open	Method (window object)	193
parent	Property	193
parse	Method	193
parseFloat	Function	194
parseInt	Function	194
password	Object	194
pathname	Property	195
PI	Property	195
port	Property	196
pow	Method	196
prompt	Method	196
protocol	Property	197
radio	Object	197
random	Method	198
referrer	Property	198
reset	Object	199
return	Programming Keyword	200
round	Method	200

Tag	Type	Page
search	Property	201
select	Method	201
select	Object (options array)	201
selected	Property	202
selectedIndex	Property	203
setDate	Method	203
setHours	Method	203
setMinutes	Method	203
setMonth	Method	204
setSeconds	Method	204
setTime	Method	204
setTimeout	Method	204
setYear	Method	205
sin	Method	205
small	Method	205
SQRT1_2	Property	205
SQRT2	Property	206
status	Property	206
strike	Method	206
string	Object	206
submit	Method	208
submit	Object	208
tan	Method	210
target	Property	210
text	Object	210
text	Property	211
textarea	Object	212
title	Property	213
toGMTString	Method	214
toLocaleString	Method	214

➡

Tag	Type	Page
unescape	Function	214
userAgent	Property	214
UTC	Method	215
value	Property	215
var	Programming Keyword	216
vlinkColor	Property	217
while	Programming Keyword	217
window	Object	218
window	Property	221
with	Programming Keyword	218
write	Method	222
writeln	Method	222

PART II: JAVASCRIPT SORTED BY TYPE

Type	Tag	Page
Event Handler	onBlur	188
	onChange	189
	onClick	189
	onFocus	190
	onLoad	190
	onMouseOver	191
	onSelect	191
	onSubmit	192
	onUnload	192
Function	escape	163
	eval	163
	isNaN	179

Type	Tag	Page
	parseFloat	194
	parseInt	194
	unescape	214
Method	abs	145
	acos	145
	alert	145
	anchor	146
	asin	148
	atan	148
	back	149
	big	149
	blink	150
	blur	150
	bold	150
	ceil	152
	charAt	152
	clear	154
	clearTimeout	155
	click	155
	close	155
	close	156
	confirm	156
	cos	157
	exp	164
	floor	165
	focus	165
	fontcolor	165
	fontsize	166
	forward	168
	getDate	170
	getDay	171

➡

Type	Tag	Page
	getHours	171
	getMinutes	171
	getMonth	171
	getSeconds	172
	getTime	172
	getTimezoneOffset	172
	getYear	172
	go	173
	indexOf	178
	italics	179
	lastIndexOf	179
	link	181
	log	185
	max	187
	min	187
	parse	193
	pow	196
	prompt	196
	random	198
	round	200
	select	201
	setDate	203
	setHours	203
	setMinutes	203
	setMonth	204
	setSeconds	204
	setTime	204
	setTimeout	204
	setYear	205
	sin	205
	small	205

Type	Tag	Page
	strike	206
	submit	208
	tan	210
	toGMTString	214
	toLocaleString	214
	UTC	215
	write	222
	writeln	222
Method (document object)	open	193
Method (window object)	open	193
Object	anchor	146
	array	147
	button	151
	checkbox	152
	Date	157
	document	160
	hidden	173
	history	175
	location	184
	Math	185
	navigator	187
	password	194
	radio	197
	reset	199
	string	206
	submit	208
	text	210
	textarea	212
	window	218
Object (forms array)	form	166
Object (frames array)	frame	169

Type	Tag	Page
Object (links array)	link	182
Object (options array)	select	201
Programming Keyword	break	151
	continue	156
	do while	162
	for	166
	function	170
	if	177
	if ... else	178
	new	188
	return	200
	var	216
	while	217
	with	218
Property	action	145
	alinkColor	146
	appCodeName	147
	appName	147
	appVersion	147
	bgColor	149
	checked	154
	cookie	156
	defaultChecked	158
	defaultSelected	159
	defaultStatus	159
	defaultValue	159
	E	162
	elements array	162
	encoding	163
	fgColor	164
	hash	173

➡

Type	Tag	Page
	host	177
	hostname	177
	href	177
	index	178
	length	180
	linkColor	181
	LN10	183
	LN2	183
	location	185
	LOG10E	185
	LOG2E	185
	method	187
	parent	193
	pathname	195
	PI	195
	port	196
	protocol	197
	referrer	198
	search	201
	selected	202
	selectedIndex	203
	SQRT1_2	205
	SQRT2	206
	status	206
	target	210
	text	211
	title	213
	userAgent	214
	value	215
	vlinkColor	217
	window	221

Appendix E

JavaScript Objects & Arrays

This appendix lists the various JavaScript objects and arrays. For each one, you will find associated properties, methods, and event handlers with a short description of what each one does. We've also noted the parent object of each.

Remember, by the way, that we are treating all objects that are descendants of another object as *properties* of that object.

ANCHOR

An HTML anchor, created using the <A NAME=> tag. It can be targeted by a link. If the anchor includes the HREF= attribute, it is also a link object.

The anchor object is a property of the document object. It has no properties, methods, or event handlers.

ANCHORS ARRAY

The anchors array is a property of the document object, and is a list of all the anchor objects in a document. If an anchor is also a link, then it appears in *both* the anchors and the links arrays.

| Properties | length | The number of anchors in the document. |

ARRAY

The array object is a new one, introduced with Netscape Navigator 3.0 beta 3, so it won't work with Netscape 2.0. It's a built-in object—not a property of another object.

Properties	length	The number of values held in the array.

BUTTON

This is a property of a form object. It's created using the <INPUT TYPE="BUTTON"> tag.

Properties	name	The tag's NAME= attribute.
	value	The tag's VALUE= attribute.

Methods	click	Simulates a mouse click on a button.

Event Handlers	onclick	

CHECKBOX

This is a property of a form object. It is created using the <INPUT TYPE="CHECKBOX"> tag.

Properties	checked	The selection state of the checkbox.
	defaultChecked	The tag's CHECKED= attribute.
	name	The tag's NAME= attribute.
	value	The tag's VALUE= attribute.

Methods	click	Simulates a mouse click on a button.

Event Handlers	onclick	

DATE

A built-in object—not a property of another object. Allows you to carry out a variety of procedures using dates and times.

Methods		
	getDate()	Looks in the Date object and returns the day of the month.
	getDay()	Returns the day of the week.
	getHours()	Returns the hours.
	getMinutes()	Returns the minutes.
	getMonth()	Returns the month.
	getSeconds()	Returns the seconds.
	getTime()	Returns the complete time.
	getTimeZoneoffset()	Returns the time-zone offset (the number of hours difference between Greenwich Mean Time and the time zone set in the computer running the script).
	getYear()	Returns the year.
	parse()	Returns the number of milliseconds in the Date string since January 1, 1970 00:00:00. (The Date object stores times and dates in the form of milliseconds since this date.) Note, however, that this method is not currently working correctly.
	setDate()	Changes the Date object's day of month.
	setHours()	Changes the hours.
	setMinutes()	Changes the minutes.
	setMonth()	Changes the month.
	setSeconds()	Changes the seconds.
	setTime()	Changes the complete time.
	setYear()	Changes the year.
	toGMTString()	Converts the Date object's date (a numeric value) to a string in GMT time, returning, for example, Weds, 15 June 1997 14:02:02 GMT (the exact format varies depending on the operating system that the computer is running).

toLocaleString()	Converts the Date object's date (a numeric value) to a string, using the particular date format the computer is configured to use.
UTC()	Use Date UTC(year, month, day, hrs, min, sec) to return that date in the form of the number of milliseconds since January 1, 1970 00:00:00. (The hrs, min, and sec are optional.)

DOCUMENT

A property of the window and frames objects; the document displayed in the window or in the frame.

Properties		
	alinkColor	The color of an active link (ALINK).
	anchor	An HTML anchor, created using the <A NAME=> tag. (This property is also an object in its own right.)
	anchors array	An array listing the document anchor objects (<A NAME=>). (This property is also an object in its own right.)
	bgColor	The document's background color (BGCOLOR).
	cookie	A piece of information stored in the cookie.txt file.
	fgColor	The document's text color (the TEXT attribute in the <BODY> tag).
	form	A form (<FORM>) in a document. (This property is also an object in its own right.)
	forms array	An array listing the form objects in the order in which they appear in the document. (This property is also an object in its own right.)
	lastModified	The date the document was last changed.
	linkColor	The color of the document's links, the LINK attribute in the <BODY> tag (links to documents that the user has not yet viewed).
	link	An <A HREF=> tag in the document. (This property is also an object in its own right.)

	links array	An array of the link objects in a document, in the order in which they appear. (This property is also an object in its own right.)
	location	The URL of the currently displayed document. You can't change the document.location (as that's the location of the document currently displayed). You can, however, change window.location (replacing the current document with another). While window.location *is* also an object in its own right, document.location is *not*.
	referrer	The URL of the document containing the link that the user clicked on to get to the current document.
	title	The document's title (<TITLE>).
	vlinkColor	The text color of links pointing to documents that the user has viewed. The VLINK attribute of the <BODY> tag.
Methods	clear	Clears the contents of the specified document.
	close	Closes the document stream.
	open	Opens the document stream.
	write	Writes text to the document.
	writeln	Writes text to the document, and ends with a newline character.

ELEMENTS ARRAY

A property of the form object. An array listing the elements in a form, in the order in which they appear.

Properties	length	The number of elements in the form.

FORM

A property of the document object. A form within the document.

Properties

action	A string containing the destination URL for a form submission.
button	A button in a form, created using the <INPUT TYPE="BUTTON"> tag. (This property is also an object in its own right.)
checkbox	A checkbox, created using the <INPUT TYPE="CHECKBOX"> tag. (This property is also an object in its own right.)
elements array	An array listing form elements in the order in which they appear in the form. (This property is also an object in its own right.)
encoding	The MIME encoding of the form.
hidden	A hidden (<INPUT TYPE="HIDDEN">) element in a form. (This property is also an object in its own right.)
length	The number of elements in the form.
method	How data input into a form is sent to the server; the METHOD attribute in a <FORM> tag.
radio	A radio button set (<INPUT TYPE="RADIO">) in a form.(This property is also an object in its own right.)
reset	A reset button (<INPUT TYPE="RESET">) in a form. (This property is also an object in its own right.)
select	A selection box (<SELECT>) in a form. (This property is also an object in its own right.)
submit	A submit button (<INPUT TYPE="SUBMIT">) in a form. (This property is also an object in its own right.)
target	The name of the window that displays responses after a form has been submitted.
text	A text element in a form (<INPUT TYPE="TEXT">). (This property is also an object in its own right.)

	textarea	A textarea element (<TEXTAREA>) in a form. (This property is also an object in its own right.)
Methods	submit	Submits a form (the same as using the Submit button).
Event Handlers	onsubmit	

FORMS ARRAY

A property of the document object. An array that lists the forms in the order in which they appear in the document.

Properties	length	The number of forms in the document.

FRAME

A property of the window object. A frame within the window. A frame object functions in the same way as a window object, with a few exceptions.

Properties	frames array	An array listing the child frames within this frame. (This property is also an object in its own right.)
	length	The number of frames within this frame.
	name	The frame's name (the NAME attribute in the <FRAME> tag).
	parent	A synonym for the parent window containing this frame.
	self	A synonym for the current frame.
	window	A synonym for the current frame.

| Methods | clearTimeout() | Used to stop the setTimeout method from working. |
| | setTimeout() | Waits a specified number of milliseconds, then runs the instructions. |

FRAMES ARRAY

A property of both the window and frame objects. Lists the frames within the window or within the frame in the order in which they appear in the document.

| Properties | Length | The number of frames within the window or frame object. |

HIDDEN

A property of the form object. A hidden (<INPUT TYPE="HIDDEN">) element in a form.

| Properties | name | The tag's NAME= attribute. |
| | value | The tag's VALUE= attribute. |

HISTORY

A property of the window object. The window's history list.

| Properties | Length | The number of items in the history list. |

Methods	back	Loads the previous document in the history list.
	forward	Loads the next document in the history list.
	go	Loads a document in the history list, specified by its position in the list.

IMAGE

A property of the document object. An image embedded into a document with the <IMG> tag. This is a new object, introduced with Netscape Navigator 3.0 beta 3.

Properties		
	border	The tag's BORDER attribute.
	complete	A boolean value which indicates whether the browser has completely loaded the image.
	height	The HEIGHT attribute.
	hspace	The HSPACE attribute.
	lowsrc	The LOWSRC attribute.
	src	The SRC attribute.
	vspace	The VSPACE attribute.
	width	The WIDTH attribute.

Event Handlers	
	onload
	onerror
	onabort

IMAGES ARRAY

A property of the document object. A list of all the images in the document.

Properties		
	length	The number of images in the document.

LINK

A property of the document object. An <A HREF=> tag in the document.

Properties		
	hash	A string beginning with a hash mark (#) that specifies an anchor within the URL.

host	The host name part of the URL which includes a colon and the port number.
hostname	The same as the host property, except that the colon and port number are not included.
href	The entire URL.
pathname	The directory path portion of a URL.
port	The :port portion of a URL.
protocol	The URL type (http:, ftp:, gopher:, and so on).
search	Part of the URL beginning with a ? that specifies search information.
target	The window that displays the content of the referenced document when the user clicks on a link (the TARGET attribute).

Event Handlers   onclick

onmouseover

LINKS ARRAY

A property of the document object. A list of all the links in the document.

Properties   length   The number of links in the document.

LOCATION

A property of the document object. The full URL of the document. Do not confuse this with the window.location property, which can be used to load a new document. The window.location property is not an object in its own right. Also, whereas window.location can be modified by a script, document.location cannot.

Properties	hash	A string beginning with a hash mark (#) that specifies an anchor within the URL.
	host	The host name part of the URL which includes a colon and the port number.
	hostname	The same as the host property, except that the colon and port number are not included.
	href	The entire URL.
	pathname	The directory path portion of a URL.
	port	The :port portion of a URL.
	protocol	The URL type (http:, ftp:, gopher:, and so on).
	search	Part of the URL beginning with a ? that specifies search information.
	target	The window that displays the content of the referenced document when the user clicks on a link (the TARGET attribute).

MATH

This is not a property of another object; it's a built-in object. Math contains mathematical constants and functions.

Properties	E	Euler's constant and the base of natural logarithms (approximately 2.718).
	LN2	The natural logarithm of 2 (approximately 0.693).
	LN10	The natural logarithm of 10 (approximately 2.302).
	LOG2E	The base 2 logarithm of e (approximately 1.442).
	LOG10E	The base 10 logarithm of e (approximately 0.434).
	PI	The value of pi (approximately 3.14159).
	SQRT1_2	The square root of one-half (one over the square root of two approximately 0.707).
	SQRT2	The square root of two (approximately 1.414).

Methods	abs()	Returns a number's absolute value (its "distance from zero"; for instance, both 2 and -2 have absolute values of 2).
	acos()	Returns the arc cosine of a number (in radians).
	asin()	Returns the arc sine of a number (in radians).
	atan()	Returns the arc tangent of a number (in radians).
	ceil()	Returns the integer equal to or immediately above a number (ceil(-22.22) would return 22; ceil(22.22) would return 23; ceil(22) would return 22).
	cos()	Returns the cosine of a number (in radians).
	exp()	Returns e^{number}.
	floor()	The opposite of ceil. (ceil(-22.22) would return 22; ceil(22.22) would return 22; ceil(22) would return 22).
	log()	Returns the natural logarithm (base e) of a number.
	max()	Returns the greater of two numbers.
	min()	Returns the lesser of two numbers.
	pow()	Returns $base^{exponent}$.
	random()	Returns a pseudo-random number between zero and one. (This method only works on UNIX versions of Netscape Navigator.)
	round()	Returns a number which is rounded to the nearest integer.
	sin()	Returns the sine of a number (in radians).
	sqrt()	Returns the square root of a number.
	tan()	Returns the tangent of a number.

NAVIGATOR

This is not a property of another object; it is a built-in object. Information about the browser that has loaded the document.

Properties		
	appCodeName	The browser's code name (*Mozilla*, for instance).
	appName	The browser's name.
	appVersion	The browser's version number.
	userAgent	The user-agent header text sent from the client to the server.

Methods		
	javaEnabled	This method is currently not in JavaScript, but will probably be added soon. It will check to see if the browser is a JavaScript-compatible browser and, if so, whether JavaScript has been enabled.

OPTIONS ARRAY

A property of the select object. A list of all the options (<OPTION>) within the selection box.

Properties		
	defaultSelected	The default selection in the selection list.
	index	The index position of an option in the selection list.
	length	The number of options (<OPTIONS>) in the selection list.
	name	The tag's NAME= attribute.
	selected	A boolean value which indicates the selection state of an option <OPTION> in the selection list.
	selectedIndex	The index (position) of the selected <OPTION> in the selection list.
	text	The text after an <OPTION> tag in the selection list.
	value	The tag's VALUE= attribute.

PASSWORD

A property of the document object. A <INPUT TYPE="PASSWORD"> tag.

Properties	defaultValue	The default value of the password object (the VALUE= attribute).
	name	The tag's NAME= attribute.
	value	The current value held by the field. Initially it's the same as the VALUE= attribute (defaultValue), but if a script modifies the value held by the field, value will change.
Methods	focus	Moves focus from the field.
	blur	Moves focus to the field.
	select	Selects the input area.

RADIO

A property of the form object. A set of radio buttons (option buttons) in the form (<INPUT TYPE="RADIO">).

Properties	checked	The state of a checkbox or option button (radio button).
	defaultChecked	The default state of a checkbox or option button (radio button).
	length	The number of buttons in the set.
	name	The tag's NAME= attribute.
	value	The tag's VALUE= attribute.
Methods	click	Simulates a mouse click on a button.
Event Handlers	onclick	

RESET

A property of the form object. A reset button (<INPUT TYPE="RESET">)

Properties	name	The tag's NAME= attribute.
	value	The tag's VALUE= attribute.
Methods	click	Simulates a mouse click on a button.
Event Handlers	onclick	

SELECT

A property of the form object. A selection box (<SELECT>).

Properties	length	The number of options (<OPTIONS>) in the selection list.
	name	The tag's NAME= attribute.
	options	The number of options in the list.
	selectedIndex	The index (position) of the selected <OPTION> in the selection list.
	text	The text after an <OPTION> tag in the selection list.
	value	The tag's VALUE= attribute.
Methods	blur	Removes focus from the selection list.
	focus	Moves focus to the selection list.
Event Handlers	onblur	
	onchange	
	onfocus	

STRING

This is not a property of another object; it is a built-in object. A series of characters. Strings are entered into a script between quotation marks.

Properties	length	The number of characters in the string.
Methods	anchor()	Used to turn the string into an HTML anchor tag (<A NAME=).
	big()	Changes the text in the string to a big font (<BIG>).
	blink()	Changes the text in the string to a blinking font (<BLINK>).
	bold()	Changes the text in the string to a bold font (<B>).
	charAt()	Finds the character in the string at a specified position.
	fixed()	Changes the text in the string to a fixed-pitch font (<TT>).
	fontcolor()	Changes the text in the string to a color (<FONT COLOR=>).
	fontsize()	Changes the text in the string to a specified size (<FONTSIZE=>).
	indexOf()	Used to search the string for a particular character, and returns the index position of that character.
	italics()	Changes the text in the string to italics (<I>).
	lastIndexOf()	Like indexOf, but searches backward to find the last occurrence of the character.
	link()	Used to turn the string into an HTML link tag (<A HREF=).
	small()	Changes the text in the string to a small font (<SMALL>).
	strike()	Changes the text in the string to a strikethrough font (<STRIKE>).

sub()	Changes the text in the string to a subscript font (<SUB>).
substring()	Returns a portion of the string between specified positions within the string.
sup()	Changes the text in the string to a superscript font (<SUP>).
toLowerCase()	Changes the text in the string to lowercase.
toUpperCase()	Changes the text in the string to uppercase.

SUBMIT

A property of the form object. A submit button in the form (<INPUT TYPE="SUBMIT">).

Properties	name	The tag's NAME= attribute.
	value	The tag's VALUE= attribute.
Methods	click	Simulates a mouse click on a button.
Event Handlers	onclick	

TEXT

A property of the form object. A text field in the form (<INPUT TYPE="TEXT">).

Properties	defaultValue	The default value of the text object (the VALUE= attribute).
	name	The tag's NAME= attribute.
	value	The current value held by the field. Initially, it's the same as the VALUE= attribute (defaultValue), but if a script modifies the value held by the field, value will change.

Methods	blur	Removes focus from the text box.
	focus	Moves focus to the text box.
	select	Selects the input area.

Event Handlers	onblur
	onchange
	onfocus
	onselect

TEXTAREA

A property of the form object. A textarea field in the form (<TEXTAREA>).

Properties	defaultValue	The default value of the textarea object (the VALUE= attribute).
	name	The tag's NAME= attribute.
	value	The current value held by the field. Initially, it's the same as the VALUE= attribute (defaultValue), but if a script modifies the value held by the field, value will change.

Methods	blur	Removes focus from the textarea.
	focus	Moves focus to the textarea.
	select	Selects the input area.

Event Handlers	onblur
	onchange
	onfocus
	onselect

WINDOW

This is not a property of another object; it is the top-level object. The browser window.

Properties	defaultStatus	The default status bar message.
	document	The currently displayed document. (This property is also an object in its own right.)
	frame	A frame (<FRAME>) within a window. (This property is also an object in its own right.)
	frames array	An array listing the window's frame objects in the order in which they appear in the document. (This property is also an object in its own right.)
	history	The window's history list. (This property is also an object in its own right.)
	length	The number of frames in the window.
	location	The full (absolute) URL of the document displayed by the window. (This property is also an object in its own right.)
		Don't confuse this with document.location, which is the URL of the currently displayed document. You can change window.location (replacing the current document with another), but you can't change the document.location (as that's the location of the document currently displayed).
	name	The name assigned to the window when opened.
	opener	Refers to the window in which a script used window.open to open the current window. This is a new property, introduced with Netscape Navigator 3.0 beta 3.
	parent	A synonym for the window containing the current frame. Also a property of the frame object.
	self	A synonym for the current window or frame.
	status	A message in the status bar.
	top	A synonym for the top-most browser window containing the current frame.

	window	A synonym for the current window or frame. The same as self.
Methods	alert()	Opens an Alert message box.
	clearTimeout()	Used to stop the setTimeout method from working.
	close()	Closes the window.
	confirm()	Opens a Confirm message box; the user has two choices, OK and Cancel—the method returns true if the user clicks on OK, false if on Cancel.
	blur()	Moves the focus away from the specified window. This is a new method, introduced in the Netscape Navigator 3.0 beta 3.
	focus()	Brings the specified window to the foreground. (Another new method.)
	open()	Opens a new window.
	prompt()	Opens a Prompt dialog box; the user can type into this box and the typed text is returned to the script.
	setTimeout()	Waits a specified number of milliseconds, then runs the instructions.
Event Handlers	onload	
	onunload	

Appendix F
JavaScript Properties

Properties are related to objects. Many properties work with multiple objects. This Appendix is a quick summary of the different properties available. It's a good idea to read through this list simply to get an idea of what's available to you.

The list tells you which object or objects may use each property. (See Appendix E, "JavaScript Objects & Arrays" for more information about each object and its related properties, methods, and event handlers.) Remember, many properties are objects in their own right; they have their own properties. We've indicated which properties are also objects.

A quick word about what you'll find when you go looking for more information. The Netscape JavaScript Authoring Guide (see Appendix J, "Finding More Information," for the source of this documentation) has a properties table, but it doesn't list all the items that we have treated as properties. Remember that there are objects that are descendants of another object, yet which function independently of that object. For simplicity's sake we have chosen to treat all descendants of an object as properties. So while, for instance, it could be argued that an anchor object is not, strictly speaking, a property of the document object, it *is* a descendant of the document object. The distinction between a property of an object and an object that is a descendant of another object yet not a property of that object is not particularly important, so we regard the anchor as a property of the document object.

Of course a number of objects are not properties; Date, Math, Array, navigator, and string objects are "built-in" objects—objects that are available from anywhere because they are not related to other objects.

action	A string that contains the destination URL for a form submission. A property of the form object.
alinkColor	The color of an active link (ALINK). A property of the document object.
anchor	An HTML anchor, created using the <A NAME=> tag. A property of the document object. (This property is also an object in its own right.)
anchors array	An array which lists the document anchor objects (<A NAME=>). A property of the document object.
appCodeName	The browser's code name (*Mozilla*, for instance). A property of the navigator object.
appName	The browser's name. A property of the navigator object.
appVersion	The browser's version number. A property of the navigator object.
bgColor	The document's background color (BGCOLOR). A property of the document object.
border	The <IMG> tag's BORDER attribute. A property of the image object. This is a new property, introduced with Netscape Navigator 3.0 beta 3.
button	A button in a form, created using the <INPUT TYPE="BUTTON"> tag. A property of the form object. (This property is also an object in its own right.)
checkbox	A checkbox, created using the <INPUT TYPE="CHECKBOX"> tag. A property of the form object. (This property is also an object in its own right.)
checked	The state of a check box or option button (radio button). A property of the checkbox object and the radio object.

complete	A boolean value which indicates whether the browser has completely loaded an image. A property of the image object. This is a new property, introduced with Navigator 3.0 beta 3.
cookie	A piece of information stored in the cookie.txt file. A property of the document object.
defaultChecked	The default state of a check box or option button (radio button). A property of the checkbox object and the radio object.
defaultSelected	The default selection in a selection list (<SELECT>). A property of the select object.
defaultStatus	The default status-bar message. A property of the window object.
defaultValue	The default value of a password, text, or textarea object (the VALUE= attribute). A property of the hidden, password, text, and textarea objects.
document	The currently displayed document. A property of the window and frame objects. (This property is also an object in its own right.)
E	Euler's constant and the base of natural logarithms (approximately 2.718). A property of the Math object.
elements array	An array that lists form elements in the order in which they appear in the form. A property of the form object.
encoding	The MIME encoding of the form. A property of the form object.
fgColor	The document's text color (the TEXT attribute in the <BODY> tag). A property of the document object.
form	A form (<FORM>) in a document. A property of the document object. (This property is also an object in its own right.)
forms array	An array that lists the form objects in the order in which they appear in the document. A property of the document object.

frame	A frame (<FRAME>) within a window. A property of the window object. (This property is also an object in its own right.)
frames array	An array that lists the window's frame objects in the order in which they appear in the document. A property of the window object.
hash	A string beginning with a hash mark (#) that specifies an anchor within the URL. A property of the location and link objects.
height	The HEIGHT attribute of an <IMG> tag. A property of the image object. This is a new operator, introduced with Netscape Navigator 3.0 beta 3).
hidden	A hidden (<INPUT TYPE="HIDDEN">) element in a form. A property of the form object. (This property is also an object in its own right.)
history	The window's history list. A property of the window object. (This property is also an object in its own right.)
host	The hostname part of the URL that includes a colon and the port number. A property of the location and link objects.
hostname	The same as the host property, except that the colon and port number are not included. A property of the location and link objects.
href	The entire URL. A property of the location and link objects.
hspace	The HSPACE attribute of the <IMG> tag. A property of the image object. This is a new property, introduced with Netscape Navigator 3.0 beta 3.
image	An image embedded with the <IMG> tag. A property of the document object. (This property is also an object in its own right.) This is a new property, introduced with Netscape Navigator 3.0 beta 3.
images array	An array that lists the embedded image objects. A property of the document object.

index	The index position of an option in a selection list (<SELECT>). A property of the options array.
lastModified	The date the document was last changed. A property of the document object.
length	A number that is related to the object or array using the property, such as a number of elements in a form or the number of frames in a window. A property of the frame, history, radio, select, string, and window objects; and a property of the anchors, elements, forms, frames, links, options, and images arrays.
linkColor	The color of the document's links. The LINK attribute in the <BODY> tag (links to documents that the user has not yet viewed). A property of the document object.
link	An <A HREF=> tag in the document. A property of the document object. (This property is also an object in its own right.)
links array	An array of the link objects in a document, in the order in which they appear. A property of the document object.
LN2	The natural logarithm of 2 (approximately 0.693). A property of the Math object.
LN10	The natural logarithm of 10 (approximately 2.302). A property of the Math object.
location	The full (absolute) URL of the document displayed by the window. A property of the window object. (This property is also an object in its own right.) Also, a property of the document object. The URL of the currently displayed document. Thus you can change window.location (replacing the current document with another), but you can't change the document.location (as that's the location of the document currently displayed). While window.location *is* also an object in its own right, document.location is *not*.
LOG2E	The base 2 logarithm of e (approximately 1.442). A property of the Math object.

LOG10E	The base 10 logarithm of e (approximately 0.434). A property of the Math object.
lowsrc	The LOWSRC attribute of an <IMG> tag. A property of the image object. This is a new property, introduced with Netscape Navigator 3.0 beta 3.
method	How data input in a form is sent to the server; the METHOD attribute in a <FORM> tag. A property of the form object.
name	The name (the NAME= attribute) of an object. A property of button, checkbox, frame, hidden, password, radio, reset, select, submit, text, and textarea objects, and the options array. For the window object, name is the name assigned to the window when opened.
opener	Refers to the window in which a script used window.open to open the current window. A property of the window object. This is a new property, introduced with Netscape Navigator 3.0 beta 3.
options array	An array of the options (<OPTION>) in a selection list (<SELECT>), in the order in which they appear. A property of the select object.
password	A password (<INPUT TYPE="PASSWORD") object in a form. A property of the form object. (This property is also an object in its own right.)
parent	A synonym for the window that contains the current frame. A property of the frame and window objects.
pathname	The directory path portion of a URL. A property of the link and location objects.
PI	The value of pi (approximately 3.14159). A property of the Math object.
port	The :port portion of a URL. A property of the link and location objects.
protocol	The URL type (http:, ftp:, gopher:, and so on). A property of the link and location objects.

radio	A radio button set (<INPUT TYPE="RADIO">) in a form. A property of the form object. (This property is also an object in its own right.)
referrer	The URL of the document that contains the link that the user clicked on to get to the current document. A property of the document object.
reset	A reset button (<INPUT TYPE="RESET">) in a form. A property of the form object. (This property is also an object in its own right.)
search	Part of the URL beginning with a ? that specifies search information. A property of the link and location objects.
select	A selection box (<SELECT>) in a form. A property of the form object. (This property is also an object in its own right.)
selected	A boolean value that indicates the selection state of an option <OPTION> in a selection list (<SELECT>). A property of the options array.
selectedIndex	The index (position) of the selected <OPTION> in a selection list (<SELECT>). A property of the select object and options array.
self	A synonym for the current window or frame. A property of the frame and window objects.
SQRT1_2	The square root of one-half (1 over the square root of 2, approximately 0.707). A property of the Math object.
SQRT2	The square root of two (approximately 1.414). A property of the Math object.
src	The SRC attribute of an <IMG> tag. A property of the image object. This is a new property, introduced with Netscape Navigator 3.0 beta 3.
status	A message in the status bar. A property of the window object.
submit	A submit button (<INPUT TYPE="SUBMIT">) in a form. A property of the form object. (This property is also an object in its own right.)

target	The name of the window that displays responses after a form has been submitted; or, the window that displays the content of the referenced document when the user clicks on a link (the TARGET attribute). A property of the form, link, and location objects.
text	The text after an <OPTION> tag in a selection list (<SELECT>). A property of the options array. Also, a text element in a form (<INPUT TYPE="TEXT">). A property of the form object. (This property is an object in its own right.)
textarea	A textarea element (<TEXTAREA>) in a form. A property of the form object. (This property is also an object in its own right.)
title	The document's title (<TITLE>). A property of the document object.
top	A synonym for the top-most browser window that contains the current frame. A property of the window object.
type	A form element's TYPE= attribute or tag name. A property of text, radio, checkbox, hidden, submit, reset, password, button, select, textarea, and image objects. This is a new property, introduced with Netscape Navigator 3.0 beta 3.
typeof	Returns a string that tells the type of its unevaluated operand. This is a new operator, introduced with Netscape Navigator 3.0 beta 3.
userAgent	The user-agent header text sent from the client to the server. A property of the navigator object.
value	The current value held by the related object. Initially it's the same as the VALUE= attribute (defaultValue), but if the user or a script modifies the value held by the object then value will change. A property of the button, checkbox, hidden, password, radio, reset, submit, text, and textarea objects and the options array.

vlinkColor — The text color of links pointing to documents that the user has viewed. The VLINK attribute of the <BODY> tag. A property of the document object.

vspace — The VSPACE attribute of an <IMG> tag. A property of the image object. This is a new property, introduced with Netscape Navigator 3.0 beta 3.

width — The WIDTH attribute of an <IMG> tag. A property of the image object. This is a new property, introduced with Netscape Navigator 3.0 beta 3.

window — A synonym for the current window or frame. The same as self.

Appendix G
JavaScript Event Handlers

This appendix provides a summary of the event handlers that are available for use in JavaScript. Events are actions a user may take, such as clicking on a button or link, opening or closing a document, and moving focus to and from form elements. The event handlers are placed within HTML tags.

onabort—The JavaScript is executed if the user stops an image from loading (by clicking on the Stop button or loading another document, for instance). This works with the <IMG> tag, but it's a new event handler, introduced with Netscape Navigator 3.0 beta 3.

onblur—The JavaScript is executed when a particular form component loses focus, that is, when the component was selected (the cursor inside it, for instance) and the user moves focus to another component by clicking elsewhere or pressing Tab. The onblur event handler works with the selection list (<SELECT>), multi-line text-input (<TEXTAREA>), and text input (<INPUT TYPE="TEXT">) components.

onchange—The same as the onblur, with the exception that something must have been changed in the form components for the JavaScript to be run.

onclick—The JavaScript is executed when the user clicks on a button (<INPUT TYPE="BUTTON">), checkbox (<INPUT TYPE="CHECKBOX">), option (radio) button (<INPUT TYPE="RADIO">), a link (<A HREF=>), or a Reset (<INPUT TYPE="RESET">) or Submit (<INPUT TYPE="SUBMIT">) button.

onerror—The JavaScript is executed if an image could not be loaded. This event handler works with the <IMG> tag, but note that it's a new event handler, introduced with the Netscape Navigator 3.0 beta 3.

onfocus—Similar to the onblur, except that the focus is moving *to* the component, not away.

onload—The JavaScript is run when the page is loaded into the browser (specifically, once the browser has finished loading the page and any frames), or when an image is loaded into a document. Used within the <BODY>, <FRAMESET>, and <IMG> HTML tags. This event handler was added to the <IMG> tag with Netscape Navigator 3.0 beta 3.

onmouseover—The JavaScript executes when the user simply points at a link (<A HREF=>) with the mouse pointer.

onselect—The JavaScript is executed when the user selects text in a text (<INPUT TYPE="TEXT">) or textarea (<TEXTAREA>) form component.

onsubmit—The JavaScript is executed when the user submits a form. It's placed in the <FORM> tag, but runs when the user clicks on a submit button (the <INPUT TYPE="SUBMIT"> tag).

onunload—The JavaScript is run when the user does something to load another page into the browser—forcing unload of the current page. Used within the <BODY> and <FRAMESET> HTML tags.

Appendix H
JavaScript Reserved Words

The following words cannot be used when you are naming variables, functions, methods, or objects. Also, avoid the names of built-in objects, functions, and methods, such as, date, getdate, math, and sqrt. See Appendices E and F for a more exhaustive list. While you can sometimes use such names, you may run into a conflict.

abstract	function	super
boolean	goto	switch
break	if	synchronized
byte	implements	this
case	import	throw
catch	in	throws
char	instanceof	transient
class	int	true
const	interface	try
continue	long	var
default	native	void
do	new	while
double	null	with
else	package	
extends	private	
false	protected	
final	public	
finally	return	
float	short	
for	static	

Appendix I

Symbol Reference

It can be tricky for a newcomer to programming to keep all those little symbols straight. So here's a quick-reference table that will help you quickly identify the different symbols you'll run across while viewing JavaScripts.

+	Addition/concatenation operator; adds two numerical values together, joins two strings together.
*	Multiplication operator; multiplies two values together.
/	Division operator; divides one value by another.
%	Modulus operator; divides one value by another, then drops the digits to the right of the decimal place.
-	Subtraction operator; subtracts one value from another, or changes a value to a negative value (unary negation).
++	Increment operator; increments a value (adds one to it).
--	Decrement operator; decrements a value (subtracts one from it).
!	Boolean NOT; tells you what value the variable *doesn't* contain. X = !Y would mean that if Y is true, X is set to false, and if Y is false X is set to true.
&&	Boolean AND; "ands" two variables together. X=Y && Z, means that X is only true if Y *and* Z are both true.

|| Boolean OR. X=Y || Z, means that X is true if Y *or* Z (or both of them) are true.

^   Boolean Exclusive OR. X = Y ^ Z, means that X is set to true if Y *or* Z are true—but not if both Y *and* Z are true.

&=   Boolean AND assignment. X &= Y means that X is set to true only if X *and* Y are both true before the expression is evaluated.

^=   Boolean Exclusive OR assignment. X ^= Y means that X is set to true if X *or* Y are true—but not both true—before the expression has been evaluated.

|=   Boolean OR assignment. X |= Y, means that X is set to true if either X *or* Y are true before the expression has been evaluated.

=   Assignment operator; assigns values to variables.

+=   Addition assignment; adds the variables together, and modifies the variable on the left side.

-=   Subtraction assignment; subtracts the variable on the left from the one on the right, and modifies the variable on the left.

*=   Multiplication assignment; multiplies the variables together, then modifies the variable on the left.

/=   Division assignment; divides the variable on the left by the one on the right, then modifies the one on the left.

%=   Modulus assignment; divides the variable on the left by the one on the right, discards the digits to the right of the decimal place, and modifies the variable on the left.

<   Conditional operator. Less than.

<=	Conditional operator. Less than or equal to.
>	Conditional operator. Greater than.
>=	Conditional operator. Greater than or equal to.
==	Conditional operator. Equal to.
!=	Conditional operator. Not equal to.
?:	Shorthand if statement operator, or ternary operator (? is used in combination with :, as in variable = (condition) ? value1 : value2).
" "	Double-quotation marks—enclose string literals, and instructions in event handlers.
' '	Single-quotation marks—enclose string literals when the statement is already enclosed in double-quotation marks.
;	Separates individual statements within a function.
.	Divides up parts of object property or method name (e.g., document.write).
,	Separates parameters and features within feature list.
( )	Enclose parameters (arguments) after function name, and set operator precedence.
[]	Enclose item position number in array.
{ }	Enclose blocks of script within statements, functions, and loops.
~	Bitwise complement.

`<<=`	Bitwise left shift assignment.
`&`	Bitwise operator, And.
`<<`	Bitwise operator, left shift.
`|`	Bitwise operator, Or.
`>>`	Bitwise operator, right shift.
`^`	Bitwise operator, Xor.
`>>>`	Bitwise operator, zero-fill right shift.
`>>=`	Bitwise right shift assignment.
`>>>=`	Bitwise zero fill right shift assignment.
`<!--` `//-->`	HTML comment tags, used in JavaScripts to hide scripts from non-JavaScript browsers; everything between the symbols is ignored by non-JavaScript browsers.
`//`	JavaScript comment line; everything to the right of the symbol is assumed to be a comment and ignored.
`/*` `*/`	JavaScript comment block; everything between the asterisks is assumed to be a comment and ignored.

Appendix J
Finding More JavaScript Information

This appendix lists a variety of sources of JavaScript information.

NETSCAPE'S JAVASCRIPT AUTHORING GUIDE

You must get a copy of Netscape's JavaScript Authoring Guide. It contains a wealth of information, all the funky little details you really need to work with the various objects, properties, methods, and so on.

You can currently find the documentation covering the Netscape 2.0 version of JavaScript at

`http://www.netscape.com/eng/mozilla/2.0/handbook/javascript/`

or

`http://home.netscape.com/eng/mozilla/Gold/handbook/javascript/`

Here's the documentation for Netscape 3.0 JavaScript:

`http://home.netscape.com/eng/mozilla/3.0/handbook/javascript/`

You can also download the documentation from Netscape to your hard disk, though it's not always up to date. There's currently a link at the bottom of the Contents frame in the 2.0 version documentation, or try

`http://home.netscape.com/eng/mozilla/Gold/handbook/javascript/jsdoc.zip.`

The documentation is currently in ZIP format.

You can also find the Netscape documentation in a variety of other formats, though not always completely up to date:

JavaScript Authoring Guide in WinHelp Format

http://www.jchelp.com/javahelp/javahelp.htm

The Netscape documents placed into a Windows Help file.

JavaScript Authoring Guide in Adobe Acrobat (PDF)

http://www.ipst.com/docs.htm

This site has the authoring guide in Adobe Acrobat (PDF) format.

OTHER DOCUMENTATION

Here are some other documents that may be useful:

Introduction to JavaScript by Stefan Koch (was known as "Voodoo")

http://rummelplatz.uni-mannheim.de/~skoch/js/script.htm

This Danish site contains good tutorials, plus background info and useful links. It's also mirrored at the following US and Australian sites, respectively.

http://www.webconn.com/java/javascript/intro/

http://www.pride-web.com.au/pride/java_script/script.htm

Persistent Client State HTTP Cookies Preliminary Specifications

http://www.netscape.com/newsref/std/cookie_spec.html

Background information about working with cookies.

The JavaScript FAQ

http://www.freqgrafx.com/411/jsfaq.html

Frequently asked questions about JavaScript. Useful information on JavaScript bugs, too.

Web Interactivity: JavaScript, CGI facilitate Dynamic Web Pages

http://www.ostrabo.uddevalla.se/dis/javascript/man874p.html

A brief explanation of the differences between client-based JavaScript and server-based Common Gateway Interface (CGI).

JAVASCRIPT LIBRARIES

Here are a few JavaScript libraries from which you can borrow scripts:

JavaScript 411

http://www.freqgrafx.com/411/

The JavaScript Library at the JavaScript Index

http://www.c2.org/~andreww/javascript/lib/

JavaScript: Simple Little Things To Add To Your Pages

http://tanega.com/java/java.html

JavaScript Sweden, JavaScript Source Codes

http://www.ostrabo.uddevalla.se/dis/javascript/source.html

The JavaScript Archive

http://planetx.bloomu.edu/~mpscho/jsarchive/

JavaScript Applets

http://www.oz.net/~alden/javascript/jsintro.html

Timothy's JavaScript Page

http://www.essex1.com/people/timothy/index.html

You may find more libraries listed at the **JavaScript Index**

http://www.c2.org/~andreww/javascript/collections.html

RESOURCE SITES

These are currently the best JavaScript link sites:

Gamelan JavaScript List:

http://www.gamelan.com/noframe/Gamelan.javascript.html

Lots of JavaScript stuff. Gamelan has a Java list, too.

The JavaScript Index:

http://www.c2.org/~andreww/javascript/

Links to many JavaScript samples and resources.

Yahoo's JavaScript Category:

http://www.yahoo.com/Computers_and_Internet/Languages/
JavaScript/

Not as much stuff as the last two sites, but pretty good nonetheless.

Here are other JavaScript sites worth checking on. Not so many links, but often good examples, tutorials, and so on:

Netscape's JavaScript Introduction page:

http://www.netscape.com/comprod/products/navigator/
version_2.0/script/

An introductory promotional page for JavaScript, with links to the authoring guide and resources page.

Netscape's JavaScript Resources page:

http://www.netscape.com/comprod/products/navigator/
version_2.0/script/script_info/

A small list of links to example JavaScripts and JavaScript resources.

Unofficial JavaScript Resource Center:

http://www.intercom.net/user/mecha/java.html

Useful samples, loads of links.

LiveSoftware's JavaScript Resource Center:

`http://jrc.livesoftware.com/`

JavaScript examples, two newsgroups, and a chat room.

JavaScript 411:

`http://www.freqgrafx.com/411/`

Very useful site. It has a snippets library (take bits of JavaScript code for your Web pages), the JavaScript FAQ, and tutorials.

JavaScript Sweden Site:

`http://www.ostrabo.uddevalla.se/dis/javascript/`

Another very useful site. Contains tutorials, library, and documentation, including a mirror of documentation from Netscape Communications.

TeamJava's Home Page:

`http://www.teamjava.com/`

Java and JavaScript consultants, plus lots of links to JavaScript stuff.

Eric's JavaScript Page

`http://www.pass.wayne.edu/~eric/javascript/`

A small JavaScript links page.

DISCUSSION GROUPS

The JavaScript Mailing List

There is an unofficial repository of information in the form of a mailing list for people interested in JavaScript. For more information about the list or to view old messages point your Web browser to

`http://www.obscure.org/javascript/`

To join, send e-mail to **majordomo@obscure.org** with this in the body of the message: **subscribe javascript**.

To get a digest—a single message each day containing all the list's messages pasted together—send e-mail to **majordomo@obscure.org** with the following in the body of the message: **subscribe javascript-digest.**

Java Message Exchange

```
http://porthos.phoenixat.com/~warreng/WWWBoard/wwwboard.html
```

A Web-based discussion group.

Internet Relay Chat

The #javascript channel on Internet Relay Chat is used for JavaScript discussions.

Netscape's JavaScript Newsgroup

This newsgroup is on the secnews.netscape.com secure newserver. However, it's currently a private group, only available to members of the Development Partners program (see http://developer.netscape.com/index.html for more information).

```
snews://secnews.netscape.com/netscape.devs-javascript
```

Netscape's LiveWire Newsgroup

Netscape also has a LiveWire newsgroup; again, only for the Developers.

```
snews://secnews.netscape.com/netscape.devs-livewire
```

Java Message Exchange

A Web-based discussion group.

```
http://porthos.phoenixat.com/~warreng/WWWBoard/wwwboard.html
```

comp.lang.javascript Newsgroup

This newsgroup is available at many local news servers.

LiveSoftware's JavaScript Newsgroups

JavaScript Development Group

```
news://news.livesoftware.com/livesoftware.javascript.developer
```

JavaScript Examples Group

`news://news.livesoftware.com/livesoftware.javascript.examples`

Go to the LiveSoftware news server (news.livesoftware.com) to participate in these newsgroups. In Netscape, for instance, just type the full URL—news://news.livesoftware.com/livesoftware.javascript.examples, for instance—into the Location box and press Enter to open the Newsgroup window, connect to the server, and open the newsgroup. For more information, go to the LiveSoftware site:

`http://jrc.livesoftware.com/`

LiveSoftware's JavaScript Chat Room

`http://jrc.livesoftware.com/chat.html`

For more information about JavaScript chat, newsgroups, and mailing lists, see the JavaScript Index:

`http://www.c2.org/~andreww/javascript/.`

Glossary

As does every specific profession in the world of computing, Web programming/authoring and the Internet come resplendent with terms and acronyms that only a rocket scientist or computer geek could love. Let's not forget that many of us are new to computing because of the Internet or have just broken into cyberspace in the last year or so. For those of you who have been around since the early eighties, note that I really have done my best to omit very old (but common) terms like "bedrock" and "wheel"—but include a lot of recently introduced acronyms such as "IHMO."

As you work and participate in the evolving world of cyberspace, you'll come across terms with which you're unfamiliar. This glossary has been expanded well beyond the scope of this book to provide you with a reference that makes monthly magazine glossaries pale by comparison.

16-bit—Of hardware and software that can handle data in words that are two bytes (16 bits) wide.

32-bit—Of hardware and software that can handle data in words that are 32 bits wide.

64-bit—Of hardware and software that can handle data in words that are 64 bits wide.

access time—The amount of time it takes a hardware device (like a RAM chip or hard drive) to locate (access) one bit of data.

account—An area restricted for the use of a specific person or group of persons. An account is also a pointer into a security policy related to that person or group.

activate—To bring a window to the front of your screen and make it the window in which you are working.

active printer—The printer that will be used by programs.

active window—The window that is currently being used in the foreground of your screen.

administrator—The person responsible for a network.

agent—A program that acts in your stead. Agents usually perform mundane, repetitive tasks and are utilized by people to save time and energy.

alert message—A critical warning, confirmation, or information message. On computers that have windowing operating systems (such as Windows, Win95, X-, and Macintosh) these messages appear in dialog boxes and usually must be actively acknowledged before they will go away.

alias—An alternate name for something. In computers and in networking, aliases allow you to type fewer characters, to avoid complex hexadecimal numbers, or to know a pathname. In HTML programming, an alias may be an alternate name for a font or Latin01 characters. In the domain name system, electronic mailers, and other network software, aliases frequently are used to represent domain names or e-mail addresses in a simpler or more desirable manner.

America Online—A commercial online service that gives its subscribers access to the Internet in addition to its own body of content.

analog—Of a form of electronic information transfer that uses a continuous electromagnetic waveform rather than a digital form utilizing a series of binary digits. Broadcast TV (as opposed to cable) is accomplished by analog data transfer.

anchor—In a hypertext document, a link to another section of the document you are viewing.

angle—The degree of tilt of the vertical lines of a character (see also italic, oblique).

ANSI—Abbreviation for the *American National Standards Institute* character code system, used by Windows. It includes 256 possible character positions (see also ASCII).

ANSI.SYS—A DOS device driver used to enhance the capabilities of a PC's keyboard and monitor.

API—Abbreviation for *Application Programming Interface*. A set of interface functions available to applications.

applet—A program with single or limited functions. Many Windows and Win95 special function programs are called applets, and, from that usage, simple Java programs are also called applets.

application—Software that you use to perform a specific type of work (for example, word processing).

Archie—A program that gives you the ability to search for information at anonymous FTP sites on the Internet.

archive—An area where files are stored at an Internet site. Archives can be either public (open to everyone) or private (restricted in access).

ARPA—Abbreviation for *Advanced Research Projects Agency*. The government agency that first funded the ARPANET.

ARPANET—A network that eventually developed into the Internet (see also ARPA).

ARQ—Abbreviation for *Automatic Repeat Request*. A general term for error-control protocols featuring hardware detection and retransmission of defective data.

array—A collection of data, and an essential programming tool. Often thought of as a multidata variable. Use one name for an array (rather than 10, 100, or 500 variable names), then place all the information into the array.

article—A message submitted to a Usenet newsgroup. A newsgroup message goes to directories that can be read by various people.

ASCII—ASCII is most commonly referred to in the context of the ASCII character set, in which there are 256 characters. Text communications must be composed of characters that exist in the ASCII character set (see also binary).

ASCII file—Same as a text file.

associate—To link a document with the program that was used to create it so that both can be opened with one command.

asynchronous—Of data transmission in which actual data bytes are each preceded by a start bit and followed by a stop bit to define them when the time between transmitted characters varies.

attribute—A property or characteristic of a file. Also, an identifying characteristic of a character, which may be its font, size, style, or color.

AUP—Abbreviation for *acceptable use policy*. The restrictions that the administrators of a network segment place on the traffic the network carries.

auto answer—A modem feature that enables detection of a ring and answering without assistance from a program or human.

AUTOEXEC.BAT—A special file that automatically executes commands when you start your DOS or Windows system.

backbone—The primary or core lines of a communications network.

background operation—A job being performed by a program when another program is running in the active window or as a TSR.

baud—Rate of serial data transfer (see also BPS).

baud rate—The number of discrete signal events per second occurring on a communications channel. The number of bits per second (BPS) is often referred to as the baud rate, a usage that is technically inaccurate but widely accepted.

BBS—Abbreviation for *bulletin board service*. A computer that allows you to upload and download files and leave messages for others.

bezier—A mathematically constructed curve, such as that used in drawing programs.

binary—Of data made up of digits. Spreadsheets and word-processing files are binary files.

binary file—Any file that contains characters other than text.

bit—A bit is one-eighth of a byte, represented by either a positive or negative (on/off) electronic charge.

bitmap—A font or a graphic composed of a pattern or "map" of bits. Also referred to as a screen page in memory.

BITNET—Abbreviation for *Because It's Time Network*. A legacy network used by some universities. BITNET now runs over TCP/IP network protocols.

black—Of an extremely bold character or font.

BMP—One file extension for a bitmapped graphic.

bold—Of a character or a font with thicker lines than a regular one (see also light, medium, heavy, black).

bookmarks—Tags used by some Web browsers for marking and recalling URLs that you may frequently access. They may also be called "favorites" or collected into "hot lists."

bot—A program that watches an IRC channel (or the changes in a Web page) and then automatically responds when certain messages are entered (or changes are made to a Web page). From the term "robot."

bounce—An e-mail message that informs you of an e-mail message that couldn't be delivered.

BPS—Abbreviation for *bits per second*. Rate of serial data transfer (see also baud).

bridge—A device that links one network to another.

broken—Of a character or font with pits or cuts to suggest age or wear; they lend an "antique" effect.

browser—A program that gives you the ability to browse the World Wide Web. Some browsers offer additional functionality, such as FTP and e-mail support. Netscape Navigator[tm] is a popular browser.

BTW—Abbreviation for *by the way*. Often used in online conversations such as e-mail or news to introduce an aside or tangential thought.

buffer—A memory area used for temporary storage during input/output operations.

buffering—The method of building buffers to hold data moved to or from I/O devices such as disk drives or modems.

bullet—A character to the left of text (in an HTML document) that denotes the beginning of a new topic; it is often a bold circle but may be any shape or graphic.

bulletin board system—A host system, into which callers may dial with their modems to read and send electronic mail, upload and download files, and chat online with other callers.

byte—A data unit composed of eight bits; a number specifying a single character (see also bit).

carrier—A continuous frequency capable of being either modulated or impressed with another information-carrying signal. Carriers are generated and maintained by modems via the transmission lines of the telephone companies.

cascade—To arrange all the windows on your screen so that they are neatly stacked, with only the title bars showing behind the active window.

CERN—The European Laboratory for Particle Physics. The World Wide Web was first conceived at CERN.

CGI—Abbreviation for *Common Gateway Interface*. CGI is the "Swiss army knife" to authors working with forms in HTML. Simple programs called CGI "scripts" are executed by Web servers, performing functions such as HTML document searches and form-filling functions.

character-based interface—The traditional interface common to applications intended to be run from the DOS prompt. All text and images are made up of characters from the ASCII table.

check box—A small box found in forms that allows the user to pick from predefined selections by clicking on them.

click—To press and release the mouse button quickly.

client—In *client-server computing*, the "front-end" program that the user runs to connect with, and request information from, the *server* program. For most of the common Internet tools, many different client programs are designed to work in DOS, Windows, Macintosh, and UNIX environments.

client application—Any application or compiled object intended to run on a client computer.

client/server computing—The model or scheme underlying programs running on the Internet as well as other network and database software. In this design, the work of an application (such as FTP or WWW) is divided between two programs—the client (or "front end") and the server (or "back end"). The client program handles the work of connecting to the server and requesting files or information, and the server handles the work of finding and "serving up" the information (or of providing some other service, such as directing print jobs to a printer).

clip art—Pre-drawn art or icons, often provided with a graphics program for free use. Graphic designers working in paper used to buy sheets of non-copyright-protected artwork and "clip" with scissors the piece of art they wanted.

clipboard—A memory area that holds one piece of information for use in a program or to pass that information between two or more programs.

clock speed—The rate at which the computer clock (which governs the CPU speed) oscillates or runs, usually given in MHz.

coaxial cable—A type of wiring where the primary signal wire is surrounded by a shield.

code—The term used to describe instructions meant to be used by a computer. HTML and JavaScript instructions are often referred to as "code."

collapse—To hide additional directory levels below the selected directory level.

color pattern—A color selection that is made up of at least two other colors.

COM—A serial communications port, as in DOS.

command—An instruction to the computer or program. A command can be entered into the Command window, selected from a menu as one of the menu's items, or entered on a *command line*.

command line—A character-based interface where you enter a command made up of text characters.

command prompt—A screen symbol such as **C:>** that requests user input.

compiler—A program that converts the text you type in a programming language into a form that is optimized to be used by the computer.

compound document—A document file that contains embedded and linked data that was created in other kinds of applications.

compress—To compact or fit into a smaller space. Files are typically compressed to reduce the amount of time that it takes to transfer a file, or to reduce the amount of space it take to store a file.

CompuServe—A commercial online service that gives its subscribers access to the Internet in addition to its own libraries of content.

condensed—Of characters or fonts with characters that are more narrow and "high" than regular ones.

conference—An area of public messages on a bulletin board system, usually with a particular topic and, often, a conference host or moderator to guide the discussion. Also called folder, SIG (for "special interest group"), or echo.

control—Any window object that lets you interact with a program by selecting an action, inputting data, and so on.

control menu—A menu that exists in every window and that enables you to modify its parameters or take global actions.

Control Panel—A program that comes with Windows that enables you to make settings for many Windows actions, such as changing network, Internet, modem, and password settings.

Control—An input object in a form. List boxes and Submit buttons are examples of controls found in forms. Microsoft's ActiveX technology now refers to OLE objects as ActiveX "controls."

conventional memory—Also known as lower memory. This is the area of memory (0K to 640K) in which your DOS programs run.

CPS—Abbreviation for *characters per second*. A transfer rate estimated from the bit rate and the length of each character.

CRC—Abbreviation for *cyclical redundancy check*. An error-detection technique that checks each block of data as it's transmitted, ensuring that the block is received as it was transmitted.

current window—The window that you are currently using and that is in front of all other open windows.

cursor—The representation of the mouse on the screen. It may take many shapes.

cyberspace—A term used to refer to the entire collection of sites accessible electronically. If your computer is connected to the Internet, it is said to it exist in cyberspace.

dæmon—A program that performs a service or services for a server's operating system.

data transmission protocols—These are standards for modulation and transmission of data at various speeds. Some common standards are Bell 103 & V.21 for 300 bps, Bell 212A & V.22 for 1200 bps, V.22bis for 2400 bps, V.32 for 9600 bps, V.32 bis for 14,400 bps, and V.34 for 28,800 bps.

database—A file or group of related files that are designed to hold recurring data types as though the files were lists.

decorative—Of a font or character with artistic characteristics used to embellish text; for example, illuminated, broken, or cursive characters.

dedicated line—A telephone line that is used for a single purpose.

default—The action or selection that will occur if you make no choices. For example, Netscape browsers will always bring up the Netscape corporate home page as the "default home page" if you make no changes to the options.

default printer—The printer chosen for use as the standard or normal printer when more than one printer is installed.

default settings—The settings the software, modem, or other system component comes with out of the box.

Desktop—The screen area on which windows and objects are displayed.

dialog box—A box that appears on your screen to present or ask for information.

dialup—A connection that utilizes a modem and phone line to connect to other computers on the Internet.

disk buffer—A place in RAM where information going to or from a disk is placed temporarily. The buffers are scanned prior to seeking that same data on the disk. Disk buffers work like a disk cache, but they are less intuitive, so they are not as fast as disk caches.

disk cache—A part of RAM that is set aside to temporarily hold data read to or from a disk.

disk operating system—Also known as DOS. The disk operating system manages basic system functions such as reading a disk, saving a file, or managing the use of memory.

display—Of a font or character intended for use in large sizes, such as headlines.

DLL—Abbreviation for *dynamically linked library*. A collection of program functions in a file that can be accessed by Windows applications as needed.

DNS—An abbreviation for *Domain Name System*. The naming system that specifies the Internet IP address and an Internet host name.

DOC—A file extension for a document file; since many word processors use this extension, it does not imply a single-file format.

document window—The window that a document appears in.

domain—The name of an entity on the Internet. Outside of the U.S., domain names are suffixed with the two-digit code that indicates nationality, such as AU for Australia. In America, domain names can also be suffixed to indicate that the entity is of the government, a company, an educational institution, etc.

DOS variables—Placed in the environment area, these variables, such as FILES, BUFFERS, STACKS, and TEMP, customize how DOS works.

dot-matrix—Of a printer that uses a set of pins impacting through a ribbon onto paper to produce characters or images.

double-click—To press the mouse button twice in rapid succession while keeping the mouse still between clicks.

download—To transfer a file from a remote computer to your own local computer.

downloadable fonts—Fonts that reside on your hard disk and that are sent to the printer as needed.

dpi—Abbreviation for *dots per inch*. The number of dots on a linear inch of paper, or on a video display; a higher number implies greater quality and accuracy (see also resolution).

drag—To move an object on the screen from one place to another by clicking on it and holding down the mouse button while you move the mouse and the object of interest.

driver—A program that allows applications to link with or use a device such as a scanner, a modem, a printer driver, or a mouse driver.

drop-down list—An item found in dialog boxes and on menus that shows only one entry until its drop-down arrow icon is clicked.

dropped capital—A character that is much larger than the rest of the text and is inserted as the first character of a paragraph ("dropped in") for visual effect.

DTR—Abbreviation for *data terminal ready*. A signal generated by most modems indicating a connection between the DTE (computer) and the modem. When DTR is "high" the computer is connected.

ECPA—Abbreviation for *Electronic Communications Privacy Act*. A law that defines lawful and unlawful uses of electronic communications in the U.S.

EISA—Abbreviation for *Extended Industry Standard Architecture*. A bus standard that supports 32-bit data transfer.

e-mail—An electronic message sent via computer from one person to another.

e-mail address—The combination of user name and host (or domain name) separated by an @ symbol forms a complete e-mail address. Example: "myname@mycompany.com".

embedding—Placing a font or client application in a document so that it can be used by the recipient on another computer.

encapsulation—In object-oriented programming, the grouping of data and the code that manipulates it into a single object. If a change is made to an object class, all instances of that class (that is, all objects) are changed.

encryption—The process of scrambling information, usually for security reasons.

error-control protocols—These are various modem-based techniques that check the reliability of characters or blocks of data at a hardware level. Examples include MNP 2–4, V.42.

EXE—An extension for an executable DOS file (program).

executable program—A file that will start and run when one types its name at the DOS prompt and presses the Enter key, clicks on the file icon in the Windows or Macintosh file display, or puts its name in the Run window of the Windows Program Manager.

expanded font—A font with characters wider than usual. Also, a line that has wide spacing between characters.

expansion boards—Circuit boards that can be added to your system expanding the capability of your computer. For example, expansion boards can be used to add additional memory.

expression—A group of characters (like a word) that are treated as a single text "unit."

extended set—Characters in a font in addition to the ones available from the keyboard, usually including diacritical marks and foreign-language symbols.

extension—A one- to three-character addition to a filename, usually indicating the type of file or the application that created it (e.g., DOC, EXE, .hqx, .bin).

external viewer—A separate program used by a World Wide Web browser to display graphics or to play sound or video files. After downloading a particular media file, the Web browser launches the external viewer program appropriate to the type of file. Another term for external viewer is *helper application*.

FAQ—Abbreviation for *Frequently Asked (or Answered) Questions*.

fault tolerance—The ability of a system to recover from an error, a failure, or a change in environmental conditions (such as loss of power). True fault tolerance provides for fully automatic recovery without disruption of user tasks or files, in contrast to manual means of recovery such as restoring data loss with tape backup files.

field—A field is a dedicated space set aside for storing data. A field can be likened to a cell in a spreadsheet.

file server—A network computer that consists of some sort of fixed-disk array and a CPU. It's used for sharing stored data among network users.

finger—A program that seeks out information regarding users on a specified Internet host.

firewall—A software/hardware device array that provides isolation and security between one computer system or network and another. Many companies have firewalls between their internal intranets and the Internet.

flame—To communicate (usually in an e-mail message or in a newsgroup article) in a manner that would normally be unthinkable when communicating in person. Common attributes of flames are rudeness, bad language, and personal attacks. Some people might use a flame to confront.

flow control—A mechanism that compensates for differences in the speed of the flow of data to and output from a modem, printer, or computer.

FON—A file extension for a Windows bitmapped font file.

font—A set of characters having similar design, sometimes meaning a character set of only one style and size.

font cartridge—A plug-in assembly for a printer, extending the number of available fonts.

font family—A group of typefaces with similar characteristics. Common font families are Roman, Swiss, Modern, Script, and Decorative. For example, Arial, Arial Bold, Arial Bold Italic, Arial Italic, Small Fonts, and MS Sans Serif are all part of the sans serif Swiss font family.

font manager—A program that handles font functions such as creating printer and screen fonts from a scalable outline.

foreground operation—The condition of the program running in the active window.

formatting—The process of preparing a floppy disk or hard drive for use.

form—A data entry area on a Web page.

FOT—A file extension for a Windows file that references a TrueType scalable font file.

frame—A defined area for text or graphics in a document.

freeware—Computer software that may be distributed on bulletin board systems, and for which the author requests no license fee or registration fee.

FTP—Abbreviation for *file transfer protocol*. A method of transferring information over the Internet.

full duplex—Signal flow in both directions at the same time. It is sometimes used to refer to the suppression of online local echo and allowing the remote system to provide a remote echo.

FWIW—Abbreviation for *for what it's worth*. Jargon, used in Internet e-mail or chat.

FYI—An abbreviation used to infer the expression *for your information*.

gateway—A computer or program that interfaces networks that use different protocols. For example, Lotus cc:Mail users need a gateway to send their e-mail over the Internet.

gigabit—One billion bits per second.

gigabyte—A unit of data storage approximately equal to one billion bytes of data.

Gopher—An information retrieval system. There are both Gopher servers and clients; most Gopher servers are now accessed through WWW browsers.

grabber—Software that supports data exchanges to and from video memory between non-Windows apps and Windows.

group box—A collection of options grouped inside a box on your screen.

group window—A window within Program Manager that shows all the programs in one group.

GUI—Abbreviation for *graphical user interface*. A system of interacting with a user using graphics and icons instead of simply using text messages; for example, Microsoft Windows.

hacking—Breaking into code or programs without permission or explicit directions. Hackers pride themselves on their skill at getting into places they shouldn't. Most hackers break in for the fun of it, to annoy the system administrator, or to build up their "score" of systems broken into. "Crackers" are a special breed of hackers who delight in doing damage to a system over the Internet.

half duplex—Signal flow in both directions, but only one way at a time. It is sometimes used to refer to activation of local echo, which causes a copy of sent data to be displayed on the sending display.

headers—Lines of text found at the beginning of e-mail messages and newsgroup articles containing information about the source of the message or article.

heavy—Of a character or font with much thicker lines than a regular one (see also light, medium, bold, black).

Help—A program that gives you information.

high-level—Of a programming language that is understandable by humans without a great deal of technical knowledge, because the instructions resemble human language constructs.

hinting—A process in scalable font to increase the visual quality of characters at small sizes. It dynamically alters the shape of a character according to its size (see also scalable font).

home page—The first document a browser displays when it accesses a Web site. Normally, a home page is a jumping-off point to all areas of a Web site. Most, if not all, browsers can be configured to refer to a user-specified home page.

host address—A unique binary number assigned to a host on the Internet.

host name—A unique alphanumeric name for a host that corresponds to a host address.

hotlist—A list of your favorite World Wide Web sites that can be accessed quickly by your WWW browser (see bookmarks).

HTML—Abbreviation for *HyperText Mark-Up Language*. The rendering language that is used to create World Wide Web documents.

HTTP—Abbreviation for *Hypertext Transport Protocol*. One of the communications protocols used to transfer data over the Internet.

hyperlinks—See links.

hypertext—An online document that has words or graphics containing links to other documents. Usually, selecting the link area onscreen (with a mouse or keyboard command) activates these links.

I/O—Abbreviation for *input/output*.

I/O base address—An acronym for input/output base address. The lowermost portion of memory as it's assigned for use by hardware.

IAB—Abbreviation for *Internet Architecture Board*. A group of volunteers who strive to maintain the Internet.

icon—A small graphic symbol seen in Program Manager, used to represent a program or a document.

IETF—Abbreviation for *Internet Engineering Task Force*. A group of volunteer practitioners that help to develop Internet standards, user documents, and protocol implementations.

illuminated—Of a character or font with artistic embellishments such as flowers. Often used as a dropped capital (see also dropped capital).

IMHO—Abbreviation for *in my humble (or honest) opinion*. An acronym used in online conversations.

inactive window—An open window that is not currently in use.

index—In database management, an index is a file created especially for sorting your information in your preferred order.

insertion mode—A word processing mode where the information you type is inserted into existing text beginning at the current cursor position. To type over existing characters, switch to overtype mode.

insertion point—A flashing vertical line that shows where text will be inserted.

interface—The part of a software product that the user sees and works with using display and input devices such as the keyboard and the mouse.

internal font—A font stored permanently in a printer.

Internet—The term used to describe all the worldwide interconnected TCP/IP networks.

Internet Assistant—An add-on product for Microsoft Word for Windows. IA allows you to author or convert Word files as HTML documents.

Internet Explorer—A Web browser program offered by Microsoft.

InterNIC—The organization that assigns, stores, and manages Internet domain names.

Intranet—An internal network that uses Internet technology. Many companies now describe the network they use for intracompany communications as an Intranet.

IP address—Also called internet address. The unique address for each computer on the Internet. The IP address appears as a set of four numbers separated by periods; the numbers indicate the domain, the network, the subnetwork, and the actual host machine.

ISA—Abbreviation for *Industry Standard Architecture*. The legacy 16-bit bus still used by most personal computers worldwide.

ISDN—Abbreviation for *Integrated Services Digital Network*. An emerging digital communications standard, allowing faster speeds than are possible using modems over analog phone lines.

ISO—Abbreviation for *International Standards Organization*. A group of organizations that set standards for all aspects of technology, including network protocols, quality control procedures, and documentation formats.

ISOC—Abbreviation for *Internet Society*. An organization dedicated to encouraging proliferation and development of the Internet.

ISP—Abbreviation for *Internet Service Provider*. An ISP is a privately-owned company that offers access to the Internet and other areas of cyberspace for a fee.

ISV—Abbreviation for *independent software vendor*. A participant in the computing industry marketplace whose primary focus is the development of software.

italic—Of a character or a font with vertical lines angled to the right, usually with flowing and curved lines (see also oblique).

KB—An abbreviation for *kilobyte*. A unit of memory or storage equal to 1,024 bytes (see also kilobyte, byte).

kernel—The part of any operating system or application that performs basic functions like the handling of hardware. The kernel also handles the job of receiving requests and delegating tasks.

kerning—Adjusting the spacing between characters on a line; can be automatic (application-controlled) or manual (user-selected). (See also kerning pairs.)

kerning pairs—Pairs of characters in a font that are kerned (placed closer together) automatically when they occur together in a line. (See also kerning, track kerning.)

keyboard shortcut—A combination of keystrokes that initiates a menu command without dropping the menu down or requiring mouse action.

keyword—A predefined word in a computer or command language; a search term used in the metacontent in HTML files to allow some search engines to better index the Web page.

kill file—A file used by some newsreader software that allows you to automatically skip posts with certain attributes (specific subject, author, and so on).

kilobyte—See KB.

knowbots—Knowledge robots. Programs that search for specific content.

labels—The different components of an Internet host name.

LAN—Abbreviation for *local area network*. A network of computers that is limited in geographical scope. Most LANs are contained within one business group or building.

landscape—Horizontal (wider than high) page orientation for printing (see also orientation, portrait).

leading—(pronounced LED-ding) Space between text lines. Distance between the bottom of one line and the bottom of the next, usually specified in points (see also point).

leased line—A dedicated phone line between two points and rented from the telephone provider, used for network communications.

light—Of a character or font with thinner lines than a regular one (see also medium, heavy, bold, black).

line spacing—Same as leading.

links—The text or graphics in an HTML document that cause a Web browser program to load another document or graphic. Special constructs in HTML allow the links to be created and your browser to act on them when you activate the link.

list box—A dialog box item that displays a list of available options.

listproc—An application that helps to automate the management of electronic mailing lists. Runs mostly on UNIX machines.

listserv—Software that automatically manage electronic mailing lists. Originated on IBM mainframes, but now runs on UNIX, IBM, and Windows NT.

local heap—A memory storage area limited to 64K in size.

local host—The computer on the desktop in front of you, as opposed to computers out on the network (see remote).

log on or **log in**—To provide a user-ID and password to gain use of the resources of a computer. Sometimes your account name will also be referred to as your "login."

low-level—Of the language of the text in a program that is closer to the computer's native language than to our own way of speaking English.

LPT—The DOS designation for a line printer port (see also COM, port).

LPT drivers—These hardware-specific drivers manage data being sent to printers.

lurking—On the Internet, a slang expression that refers to observing the activity on a mailing list, newsgroup, MUD, IRC, or other communication forum without participating actively. Many *netiquette* specialists recommend lurking in a new forum to make sure you understand what the topic is and what the rules for communications are.

macro—A miniprogram that lets you perform a sequence of actions or operations with one command. In most Windows and Macintosh programs, a sequence of keystrokes and mouse actions can be recorded so that their playback can be activated by a single keystroke or keystroke combination.

mail door—An area of a bulletin board system that creates .QWK mail packets.

mail reflector—Software that distributes messages to members of a mailing list.

mailing list—A service that forwards e-mail messages it receives to everyone on a specific list of recipients.

Majordomo—Software that automates the e-mail management tasks.

MB—Abbreviation for *megabyte*. A unit of measure equal to 1,048,576 bytes. Often referred-to as a "meg."

medium—Of a character or a font with normal-thickness lines (see also light, heavy, bold, black); also, a person who professes to communicate with deceased individuals.

megabyte—See MB.

memory—Active storage for information, consisting of microchips.

menu—A list of available choices.

menu bar—Located under the title bar in Windows, it displays the names of all the available menu lists.

menu command—A word or a phrase in a menu that, when selected, activates a function.

menu title—A title for a group of commands that, when selected, enables you to view all the commands.

method—Types of functions. Behaviors associated with the object itself and with the object's properties.

metrics—Defining aspects of a font, usually relative size and relative spacing. Sometimes also the size and file attributes.

MIME—Abbreviation for *Multipurpose Internet Mail Extensions*. An enhancement to Internet e-mail that allows for the inclusion of binary data such as word processing programs, graphics, and sound.

MIPS—An acronym for *millions of instructions per second*. A measure of processing speed that refers to the average number of machine language instructions performed by the CPU in one second.

modem—An electronic device that allows digital computer data to be transmitted via analog phone lines.

moderator—A person who reviews and screens submissions to a newsgroup or mailing list. Some IRC and chat forums also have moderators.

monospaced—Of characters or fonts with equal spacing between characters, such as Courier (see also proportional).

Mosaic—A graphical interface to the World Wide Web (WWW).

MOTD—Abbreviation for *message of the day*. A message posted daily that appears on your computer screen when you log into the system or boot your workstation.

mouse pointer—The symbol that displays where your next mouse click will occur. The mouse pointer symbol changes according to the context of the window or the dialog box it appears in.

MS-DOS—Microsoft Disk Operating System.

MSN—Abbreviation for *Microsoft Network*. An online service run by Microsoft that allows access to the Internet as well as its own content.

MUDs—Abbreviation for *Multi-User Dungeons*. Interactive games on the Internet where more than one person can play together to accomplish a set goal. MUDs are being used by businesses and educators for more than recreational purposes, because a MUD allows the participants to discuss, exchange documents, and interact in real time for very little overhead. Most public MUDs, with the notable exception of SchMOOze U, a language learning center, are game-based.

multimedia—Presenting information using more than one type of medium; for example, sound, text, and graphics.

multitasking—The concurrent management of two or more distinct tasks by a computer.

nanosecond—See Ns.

narrow—Of characters or fonts with characters that are more thin and "high" than regular ones.

NETCOM NetCruiser—A software package offered by NETCOM, for use by members of the NETCOM Internet service.

netiquette—Conventions used in communications over the Net.

netnews—A collective way of referring to the Usenet newsgroups.

Netscape Navigator—To date, the world's most popular World Wide Web browser.

network—Computers and software connected for the purpose of exchanging information.

newsreaders—Applications that let you read (and usually post) articles in Usenet newsgroups.

newsgroups—The electronic discussion groups of Usenet.

NFS—Abbreviation for *Network File System*. This is a set of protocols developed by Sun Microsystems for allowing computers running different operating systems to share files and disk storage.

NIC—Abbreviation for *Network Information Center*. A service that provides administrative information about a network. Also an acronym for Network Interface Card.

NNTP—Abbreviation for *Network News Transport Protocol*. The communications protocol used to send Usenet articles over the Internet.

nodes—Individual computers connected to a network.

Notepad—A program that comes with Microsoft Windows and enables you to view and edit text files. Many HTML authors use Notepad as well as an HTML editor to fine-tune their Web pages.

NRAM—Abbreviation for *nonvolatile random access memory*. A kind of memory chip that retains data when power to the chip is turned off. NRAM is sometimes used to store default settings in modems.

Ns—Abbreviation for *nanosecond*. A measurement of the speed at which memory chips can refresh themselves with new information. One nanosecond is equivalent to one billionth of a second. RAM chips with lower ratings (80 ns versus 120 ns) are faster.

object—Encapsulated data or types of data intended to be used in a compound document created by an application (for example, ActiveX).

object handler—A dynamic-link library for an OLE server application. This DLL acts as an intermediary between the client and server applications; for example, to improve performance when it's necessary to redraw an object in the window of the client application.

oblique—Of characters or fonts with vertical lines angled to the right. Usually refers to a sans-serif font that has been changed to italic style simply by tilting(see also sans serif).

OEM—An acronym for *original equipment manufacturer*.

OLE—Abbreviation for *Object Linking and Embedding*.

online—Existing in electronic form (as in "online documentation"). Also, connected to a network.

operating system—The software that governs the basic operation of a computer. DOS and UNIX are operating systems. Windows is not an operating system, it's an environment!

option button—A dialog box item that enables you to choose only one of a group of choices. Also called a radio button.

orientation—Page alignment for printing (see also landscape, portrait).

OTOH—Abbreviation for *on the other hand*. An acronym used in e-mail, articles, and chat that presents another, relative point of view.

output stream—A method for transferring data from programs to some external device, such as a file or a network connection.

outline font—A font stored as a set of lines and curves so that it can be scaled to be produced in any needed size (see also proportional font, scalable font).

overtype mode—A word processing mode where the information you type is placed over existing text, beginning at the current cursor position. To preserve existing characters, switch to insertion mode.

package—In a compound document, an embedded icon that contains an object, a file or part of a file, or a command.

packer—A program to compress a file or multiple files into the smallest possible single file, in part by removing extraneous space characters and other "empty space" in the original file. PKZIP, WinZip, TAR, ARC, and LHARC are packers.

packet—The basic unit of data transmission over a TCP/IP network.

paging—A technique whereby virtual address space is divided into blocks of fixed-disk space called pages, that are mapped onto any physical addresses available on the system.

parameter—A variable that affects the results of a command.

parity—Information added to check the accuracy of communication. May also be used for the printer or memory.

parse—The process by which a computer examines a set of instructions and tries to make sense of them.

paste—A function that copies data from the Clipboard into a document or file at the current insertion point.

PATH—A statement in the AUTOEXEC.BAT that provides DOS with a list of directories to search when program files are not located in the current directory.

PCL—Abbreviation for *Printer Control Language*. A complex system of codes devised by Hewlett-Packard to control printers and fonts; used in LaserJet and compatible printers.

PDL—Abbreviation for *Page Descriptor Language*. A system of commands and codes used to define appearance and placement of text and graphics on a printed page; PostScript is an example.

peer-to-peer—Of network services that run on computers working as equals. Peer-to-peer operation is different than client-server services in that neither computer is required to perform a set role at all times. Machines that are interconnected in peer-to-peer networking *may* offer services using server software, but they are not required to. Windows 95 and Windows NT are examples of computer environments (operating systems) that allow desktop computers to operate in peer-to-peer mode.

permanent font—A font downloaded to a printer and stored in its memory for all ensuing print jobs; it is lost when the printer is shut off.

permanent swap file—A file that gives Windows more effective and faster memory in 386 enhanced mode. Some Web browsers require a permanent swap file in order to run properly.

PGP—Abbreviation for *Pretty Good Privacy*. A program that encrypts files. Many people use PGP to encrypt the text of e-mail or files they are sending over the Internet to better protect their privacy.

pica—A unit of type measurement; one pica equals 6 points, or about 1/6 inch (see also point). Also used to describe a typewriter character size of about 12 points (10 characters per inch). (See also elite.)

PIF—A file that provides Windows with the information it needs to know in order to run a non-Windows program.

ping—A utility program that sends out a packet to an Internet host and then waits for a response in order both to verify server activity and to measure the time taken to complete the process.

pitch—Denotes the horizontal size of a fixed-width font in characters per inch.

pixel—One element of a graphic. Equivalent to one bit of a bitmap with color and brightness information.

plotter—A specialized printer using pens to form text and graphic images.

point—A unit of type measurement equal to about 1/72 inch (see also pica).

port—TCP/IP services such as telnet, e-mail, the World Wide Web, and FTP run on specific ports in the computer.

portrait—Vertical (higher than wide) page orientation for printing (see also orientation, landscape).

post—To send a message (article) to a Usenet newsgroup. Also refers to sending data to be processed by a CGI script or a server.

PostScript—A page descriptor language used in documents and printers. It allows high degree of control of text and graphics elements (see also PCL, PDL). The term may also refer to PostScript Type 1 fonts (see also Type 1).

PPP—Abbreviation for *Point-to-Point Protocol*. This is a protocol that lets a computer link to the Internet by calling into a service provider using a modem and a standard telephone line.

preview—A mode provided by an application to allow viewing pages as they will be printed, displayed in online Help, or in a WWW browser. Often used by DOS applications that do not have WYSIWYG displays (see also WYSIWYG).

print server—A network node, usually consisting of fixed-disk storage and a CPU, that controls one or more printers that can be shared by users.

printer buffer—A temporary storage area where printer data is transferred and held until the printer can print it. In this manner, a PC can continue working as the printer continues to print.

printer driver—A program that tells Windows how to format data for a particular type of printer.

printer font—A font contained in a printer (see also permanent font).

Prodigy—A commercial online service that gives its subscribers access to the Internet in addition to its own body of content.

program group—A way of organizing a group of icons in a window.

program window—A window that contains a program and its documents.

prompt—A query from a computer notifying the user that either more input is required or that the computer has finished the last task and is awaiting input.

property—Characteristic of an object defining its state, appearance, or value. Often used to mean a program's settings.

proportional—A font with characters of varying width (see also monospaced).

protocol—A system of rules and procedures governing communications between two devices.

provider—Someone who provides access to the Internet, or who provides disk space and server services for those who wish to publish WWW sites but do not have their own Internet-connected computers.

pt—Abbreviation for *point* (see also point).

public domain—Of computer software on which no copyright exists (usually as verified by a specific statement to that effect by the author), and that may be freely used and distributed.

query—A specific request for data or instructions.

radio button—A control that allows a user to select one choice from a set of mutually exclusive choices.

raster font—A font in which characters are stored as pixels.

rasterize—To convert a scalable outline character to a bitmap for display or printing (see also font manager).

record—A group of fields that are connected together. To remember and store a sequence of keystrokes or operations (see also macro).

relational database—A database organized in a way that allows simultaneous updating of information in all related tables when the data in only one of the related tables is edited.

remote echo—A copy of the data being received as it is returned to the sending system for display on the screen.

remote host—Another computer on the network.

remote—Pertaining to a host on the network other than the computer you now are using. Originally, the term referred to a host on the other end of the wire from you. "Local" processing is done in your terminal or PC; "Remote" processing is done by the computer at the other end.

resolution—The ability of a printer or video display to show detail. Expressed as the number of dots per square inch (dpi), and sometimes including dot size.

RFC—Abbreviation for *Request For Comments*. A document submitted to the Internet governing board to propose Internet standards or to document information about the Internet.

ring—A network configuration where a series of attached devices are connected by unidirectional transmission links to form a closed path.

rlogin—A UNIX program that allows you to log on to a remote computer. *rlogin* is not secure over Internet-connected machines.

ROM—Abbreviation for *read-only memory*. Permanent memory used by a computer or printer to store programs and data (such as fonts) so that they are always available.

roman—Regular face style, as opposed to bold or italic. Usually the term refers to serif faces.

router—At its simplest, hardware that receives an Internet packet and sends it to the next hardware in the packet's path. Modern routers also filter packets in accordance with security policies or appropriate-use policies.

sans serif—"Without serifs." Of characters lacking embellishment on the ends of lines; or fonts without serifs, such as Helvetica or Arial (see also serif).

scalability—The ability of a computing element such as a process, processor, or structure to grow seamlessly.

scalable font—A font stored as a set of lines and curves so that it can be scaled to be produced in any needed size (see also outline font).

screen font—Bitmapped characters generated for display purposes. It may be available in limited sizes and may or may not match printed characters (see also printer font).

scroll arrow—Located at either end of a scroll bar, it can be clicked to scroll the screen contents up or down.

scrollbar—An object displayed at the bottom and/or right edge of a window when the window's contents aren't completely visible.

scrollbox—A small box located in the scrollbar that shows where the visible window is located in relation to the entire document, menu, or list.

serif—An embellishment on the ends of a line forming part of a character (serifs can be bars, balls, curls, or other ornamental adaptations). Of characters or fonts with serifs (see also sans serif).

server—A computer that supports other users on a network. Also used to refer to an application that supports processing on other computers.

server application—A program that runs on a server, typically as a resource to everyone on the network.

service provider—An organization, usually commercial, that provides connections to the Internet.

session—A connection between two machines on a network or on the Internet.

SGML—Abbreviation for *Standard General Markup Language*. A rendering language that supports the presentation of information across all computer platforms.

shared resource—A printer, file, or serial computer communications device made available through the LAN to multiple computers not physically attached to the resource.

shareware—Programs or other computer materials (such as fonts, icons, and graphics) distributed at no charge, with the understanding that the user will pay for them if they continue to be used.

shortcut key—A keystroke or key combination that enables you to activate a command without having to enter into a menu.

signature—A file automatically appended to an e-mail message or newsgroup posting. New forms of signature files include a digital "key" that will let the recipient decode encrypted text or data when combined with a password already known to the recipient.

site—A group of computers or Web pages under unified administrative control.

SmartList—Software that automates the management of electronic mailing lists (see also listproc, listserv, Majordomo).

smiley face—An ASCII drawing (:-), used to indicate a positive emotion in an e-mail message.

SMTP—Abbreviation for *Simple Mail Transport Protocol*. The protocol that supports the exchange of e-mail between Internet hosts.

sockets—A software mechanism that allows programs to communicate locally or remotely by setting up endpoints for sending and receiving data.

soft font—A font downloaded to a printer when needed, usually in bitmapped format (see also scalable font, bitmap).

source code—A set of programming instructions that are compiled and linked into programs.

string—text stored in a variable.

stroke font—A font that can have its size greatly altered without distorting the font.

style—A characteristic of a font, such as bold, italic.

subscribe—To add oneself to a mailing list or newsgroup.

surfing—Moving about between sites on the World Wide Web.

symbol font—A font composed of symbols or icons rather than alphabetic or numeric characters.

sysop—The system operator of a bulletin board system.

system administrator—The person responsible for handling the day-to-day operations of a computer network.

T1—Communications lines that run at a maximum of 1.544MB per second.

T3—Communications lines that run at a maximum of 45MB per second.

table—A well-organized list of information in an HTML document.

TCP/IP—Abbreviation for *Transport Control Protocol/Internet Protocol*. A set of protocols that applications use for communicating across networks or over the Internet. These protocols specify how packets of data should be constructed, addressed, checked for errors, and so on.

temporary font—A font downloaded and then immediately discarded (see also permanent font).

terminal emulation—Running an application that lets you use your computer to interface with a command-line account on a remote computer, as if you were connected to the computer with an old-fashioned dumb terminal instead of a sophisticated computing device that may have more horsepower than the machine you're connected to.

TSR—Abbreviation for *terminate and stay resident*. Of a program that is intended to hang onto its occupied memory even after you stop running the program.

text box—A space in the dialog box where text or numbers can be entered so that a command can be carried out.

text file—A file with only text characters in it.

thread—All messages in a newsgroup that remain specific to a topic of interest.

title bar—The bar at the top of a program or a document window that shows you what its title is.

toggle—To alternate between two possible values.

traceroute—A troubleshooting utility that tells you the path between routers taken by packets moving between your host and another Internet host.

traffic—The information flowing throughout a network.

TrueType—A scalable font format devised by Apple Computer and licensed by Microsoft for use in Windows; an aspect of the TrueImage PDL.

TTF—A DOS file extension for TrueType fonts.

twisted pair—A type of cabling where pairs of communications wires are twisted together.

Type 1—A scalable font format devised by Adobe for use in PostScript printers.

Type 3—A scalable font format like PostScript Type 1 format, but without hinting. Used by some font vendors before hinting techniques became available. No longer in wide use.

typeface—A design for a collection of characters that are closely alike in design. It includes all normal styles (regular, bold, italic, bold-italic) and may include others. It does not imply size.

UNIX—An operating system used to run various types of servers.

upload—To transfer a file from your computer to another computer.

URL—Abbreviation for *Universal Resource Locator*. Specifies the location (and name) of a World Wide Web resource such as a Web site or an HTML document.

Usenet—A collection of discussion groups available via the Internet.

username—The ID used when logging onto a computer.

UUDecode—A program that converts a UUEncoded file back to its original state.

UUEncode—A program that converts binary files to text files, allowing binary information to be transmitted through gateways that are normally constrain binary files. UUEncoded files must be decoded with UUDecode before they can be accessed normally.

VAR—Abbreviation for *value-added reseller*. This term often refers to a reseller of computer products who also provides both integration and software customization services.

vector font—A font composed of lines and curves, with no interior fill. Often used by plotters.

Veronica—An Internet service that provides you with the ability to search Gopher servers.

VGA—Abbreviation for *Video Graphics Adapter*. A standard for video display 640 pixels wide by 480 pixels high, or about 72 dpi on a common monitor. Also available in Super VGA (800 by 600 pixels) and higher resolutions. Because of its worldwide adoption as a computing standard, most HTML authors create content "in VGA."

viewer—Applications or plug-ins that display or further perform a process with inbound files.

virtual—Electronic but not real in a tangible sense. "Virtual reality" is a simulation of reality using visual images and (potentially) sophisticated sensor equipment. Many people feel that the virtual world of the Internet is at least as real as their solid Earth–bound existence.

virtual device—A device that software can refer to but that doesn't physically exist.

virus—A computer program that covertly enters a system by means of a legitimate program, reproduces itself within the context of programs already running on the system, and then performs some sort of action, harmless or otherwise.

visual programming—The use of graphical development tools and visual metaphors to create software.

VRML—Abbreviation for *Virtual Reality Modeling Language*. A language that supports the display of 3D objects in HTML documents.

WAN—Abbreviation for *wide area network*, as opposed to a LAN, or local area network (which see). Citywide or statewide networks are often referred to as WANs; corporate network designers frequently refer to their corporate Intranets as WANs.

Web Crawler—A popular Web search engine.

weight—Character or font line thickness; a regular character has a lighter weight than a bold one.

WHOIS—An Internet service that displays information relative to a domain name or an e-mail address that you provide.

workstation—A terminal or personal computer, connected to a mainframe or server that by definition cannot share its own resources with other network users or the host computer.

WWW—Abbreviation for *World Wide Web*. A hypertext-based system of presenting information over the Internet.

WYSIWYG—Abbreviation for *what you see is what you get*. An acronym for an application's ability to display a document as it will be rendered to the end user.

YAHOO!—A Web indexing service and search engine that contains lists of many topics to be found on the Web.

zip—A popular method of compressing files.

the online magazine for Netscape™ users

Empower

yourself with up-to-date tools for navigating the
Net—in-depth reviews, where to find them and
how to use them.

Enhance

your online experience—get to know the latest
plug-ins that let you experience animation, video,
virtual reality and sound...live, over the Internet.

Enliven

your Web pages—tips from experienced Web
designers help you create pages with punch, spiced
with multimedia and organized for easy navigation.

Enchant

your Web site visitors—learn to create interactive
pages with JavaScript applets, program your own
Internet applications and build added functionality
into your site.

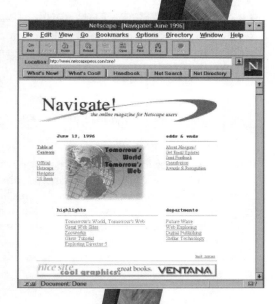

http://www.netscapepress.com/zine

Add Power to Web Pages

Official Netscape JavaScript Book

$29.99, 520 pages, illustrated, part #: 465-0

Add life to Web pages—animated logos, text-in-motion
sequences, live updating and calculations—quickly and
easily. Sample code and step-by-step instructions show how
to put JavaScript to real-world, practical use.

Java Programming for the Internet

$49.95, 806 pages, illustrated, part #: 355-7

Create dynamic, interactive Internet applications. Expand
the scope of your online development with this
comprehensive, step-by-step guide to creating Java
applets. Includes four real-world, start-to-finish tutorials.
The CD-ROM has all the programs, samples and applets
from the book, plus shareware. Continual updates on
Ventana's *Online Companion* will keep this information
on the cutting edge.

The Comprehensive Guide to VBScript

$34.99, 408 pages, illustrated, part #: 470-7

The only encyclopedic reference to VBScript and HTML
commands and features. Complete with practical examples
for plugging directly into programs. The companion CD-
ROM features a hypertext version of the book, along with
shareware, templates, utilities and more.

 Books marked with this logo include a free Internet *Online
Companion*™, featuring archives of free utilities plus a
software archive and links to other Internet resources.

Make it Multimedia

Macromedia Director 5 Power Toolkit

$49.95, 800 pages, illustrated, part #: 289-5

Macromedia Director 5 Power Toolkit views the industry's hottest multimedia authoring environment from the inside out. Features tools, tips and professional tricks for producing power-packed projects for CD-ROM and Internet distribution. Dozens of exercises detail the principles behind successful multimedia presentations and the steps to achieve professional results. The companion CD-ROM includes utilities, sample presentations, animations, scripts and files.

Shockwave!

$49.95, 400 pages, illustrated, part #: 441-3

Breathe new life into your web pages with Macromedia Shockwave. Ventana's *Shockwave!* teaches you how to enliven and animate your Web sites with online movies. Beginning with step-by-step exercises and examples, and ending with in-depth excursions into the use of Shockwave Lingo extensions, *Shockwave!* is a must-buy for both novices and experienced Director developers. Plus, tap into current Macromedia resources on the Internet with Ventana's *Online Companion*. The companion CD-ROM includes the Shockwave player plug-in, sample Director movies and tutorials, and much more!

The Comprehensive Guide to Lingo

$49.99, 700 pages, illustrated, part #: 463-4

Master the Lingo of Macromedia Director's scripting language for adding interactivity to presentations. Covers beginning scripts to advanced techniques, including creating movies for the Web and problem solving. The companion CD-ROM features demo movies of all scripts in the book, plus numerous examples, a searchable database of problems and solutions, and much more!

Follow the leader!

250,000+ in its first edition!

Hot on the heels of the runaway international bestseller comes the complete Netscape Press line—easy-to-follow tutorials; savvy, results-oriented guidelines; and targeted titles that zero in on your special interests. All with the official Netscape seal of approval!

Official Netscape Navigator Gold 3.0 Book
$39.95
Windows 420-0
Macintosh 421-9

956 pages

Official Netscape Navigator 3.0 Book
$39.99
Windows 500-2
Macintosh 512-6

696 pages

"Destined to become the bible to the world's most popular browser."
—*PC Magazine*

The definitive guide to the world's most popular Internet navigator

BY PHIL JAMES
FOREWORD BY MARC ANDREESSEN

International Bestseller!
More than 250,000 in print!

Web Favorites

Voodoo Windows 95

$24.95, 504 pages, illustrated, part #: 145-7

Users will need voodoo to make the move to Windows 95!
Nelson is back with more secrets, shortcuts and spells than
ever. Scores of tips—many never before published—on
installing, customizing, editing, printing, virtual memory,
Internet connections and much more. Organized by task
for easy reference. The companion disk contains
shareware utilities, fonts and magic!

The Windows 95 Book

$39.95, 1232 pages, illustrated, part #: 154-6

The anxiously awaited revamp of Windows means new
working styles for PC users. This new handbook offers an
insider's look at the all-new interface—arming users with
tips and techniques for file management, desktop design,
optimizing and more. A must-have for a prosperous '95!
The companion CD-ROM features tutorials, demos,
previous and online help plus utilities, screensavers,
wallpaper and sounds.

Windows 95 Power Toolkit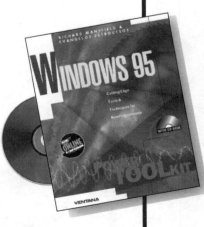

$49.95, 744 pages, illustrated, part #: 319-0

If Windows 95 includes everything but the kitchen sink, get
ready to get your hands wet! Maximize the customizing
capabilities of Windows 95 with ready-to-use tools,
applications and tutorials, including a guide to VBA. CD-
ROM: the complete toolkit, plus additional graphics, sounds
and applications.Online Companion: updated versions of
software, hyper-linked listings and links to helpful resources
on the Internet.

TO ORDER ANY VENTANA TITLE, COMPLETE THIS ORDER FORM AND MAIL OR FAX IT TO US, WITH PAYMENT, FOR QUICK SHIPMENT.

TITLE	PART #	QTY	PRICE	TOTAL

SHIPPING

For all standard orders, please ADD $4.50/first book, $1.35/each additional.
For software kit orders, ADD $6.50/first kit, $2.00/each additional.
For "two-day air," ADD $8.25/first book, $2.25/each additional.
For "two-day air" on the kits, ADD $10.50/first kit, $4.00/each additional.
For orders to Canada, ADD $6.50/book.
For orders sent C.O.D., ADD $4.50 to your shipping rate.
North Carolina residents must ADD 6% sales tax.
International orders require additional shipping charges.

SUBTOTAL = $ _____

SHIPPING = $ _____

TAX = $ _____

TOTAL = $ _____

**Or, save 15%–order online.
http://www.vmedia.com**

Mail to: Ventana • PO Box 13964 • Research Triangle Park, NC 27709-3964 ☎ 800/743-5369 • Fax 919/544-9472

Name _____

E-mail_____ Daytime phone _____

Company _____

Address (No PO Box) _____

City_____ State_____ Zip_____

Payment enclosed ___VISA ___MC ___ Acc't # _____ Exp. date_____

Signature _____ Exact name on card _____

Check your local bookstore or software retailer for these and other bestselling titles, or call toll free:

800/743-5369